THE LORD'S PRAYER

THE LORD'S PRAYER

♦

GERALD O'COLLINS SJ

PAULIST PRESS
New York/ Mahwah, N.J.

Designed by Sandie Boccacci

Phototypeset by YHT Ltd, London

This edition published by arrangement with
Darton, Longman and Todd, Ltd
1 Spencer Court
140–142 Wandsworth High Street
London SW18 4JJ

ISBN 978-0-8091-4488-4

Library of Congress Control Number: 2006938768

Published in 2007 by
Paulist Press
997 Macarthur Boulevard
Mahwah, New Jersey 07430
United States of America

Printed and bound in Great Britain

◆

CONTENTS

♦

INTRODUCTION

T HE RIVER MARNE WHICH flows north-west across central
France was the scene of an epic battle at the start of World
War I when the German forces were halted and repelled as
they advanced rapidly on Paris. Among the thousands of
soldiers who died in the early days of the Battle of the Marne
was a prophetic thinker and great poet, Charles Péguy (1873–
1914). An atheist from the age of twenty, Péguy returned to
his Catholic faith six or seven years before he died. St Joan of
Arc was his lifelong heroine, as he struggled with the sufferings that human beings endure and the hope that they can
find through the divine love. In 'A Vision of Prayer', one of
the plays found in Péguy's *Basic Verities*, it is God who comments at length on the words of the Lord's Prayer. God
introduces the opening words of the parable of the prodigal
son, and closes by declaring: 'It always ends with embraces,
and the father crying even more than anyone else.' Pro-
gressive, chant-like repetition turns God's words into an
astonishing tribute to the tender love at the heart of the 'Our
Father'.

Péguy stands with those innumerable others who for two
thousand years have cherished, prayed, proclaimed, translated, interpreted and embellished the Lord's Prayer. It has
proved a living text for public and private use, endlessly rich

for everyone in its meaning and power. It is a perfect example of what Gregory the Great said about the scriptures in general: 'they provide water in which lambs may gambol and elephants swim' (*Moralia*, dedication, 4).

Another twentieth-century poet, Edwin Muir (1887–1959), also witnessed to the enduring impact of the 'Our Father'. In March 1939 his wife, with whom he had translated several works of Franz Kafka, was seriously ill, and for the second time in his life the world was threatened with a terrible war. He found himself returning to a prayer he had learned as a boy, and it came alive with fresh power. Muir described his experience:

> Going to bed alone, I suddenly found myself (I was taking off my waistcoat) reciting the Lord's Prayer, in a loud, emphatic voice – a thing I had not done for many years – with deep urgency and profound and disturbed emotion. When I went on I became more composed; as if it had been empty and craving and were being replenished, my soul grew still; every word had a strange fullness of meaning which astonished and delighted me. It was late; I had sat up reading; I was sleepy; but as I stood in the middle of the floor half undressed saying the prayer over and over, meaning after meaning sprang from it, overcoming me again with joyful surprise; and I realized that [that] simple petition was always universal and always inexhaustible, and day by day sanctified human life.[1]

In his turmoil Muir was surprised by joy as he was flooded with new and life-giving insights from the traditional words of the 'Our Father'.

The familiar text comes from the heart of the Sermon on the Mount (Matt. 6:9–13), when Jesus teaches his disciples about prayer. Let me offer the translation which I shall follow in this book:

v. 9   Our Father in the heavens,
may your name be made holy.

v. 10 May your kingdom come, may your will be done,
on earth as in heaven.

v. 11 Give us today our daily bread.

v. 12 And forgive us our debts as we also have forgiven
our debtors.

v. 13 And do not bring us into temptation,
but deliver us from the evil one.

Luke provides a shorter version of the Lord's Prayer (Luke 11:2–4), to which I will return shortly. But it was Matthew's version which Christians took up and used.

The *Didache*, a manual for Christian conduct and worship to be dated around AD 100, followed, in a slightly edited form, Matthew's text and added: 'for yours is the power and glory for ever and ever'. Making the further additions of 'kingdom' and 'Amen', some later Christian teachers and scribes (who copied Matthew's gospel in the original Greek or in a translation) rounded off the 'doxology' or 'giving glory to God' with which many subsequent Christian versions of the 'Our Father' were to end: 'For yours is the kingdom (*basileus*), the power (*dynamis*) and the glory (*doxa*) for ever and ever. Amen.' The Septuagint or Greek OT provides sources or at least background for the doxology which the author(s) of the *Didache* and later Greek-speaking Christians added to Matthew's text. In 1 Chronicles, for instance, King David exalts God in a prayer of farewell: 'Blessed are you, O Lord, the God of our father Israel, forever and ever. Yours, O Lord, are the greatness, the power (*dynamis*), the glory (*doxa*), the victory, and the majesty; for all that is in the heavens and on the earth is yours, yours is the kingdom (*basileus*)' (29:10–11). In what was to be recognised as the closing work of the NT, the Book of Revelation had followed suit by linking 'power' and 'glory' when praising God (4:11; 7:12; 19:1) or praising Christ, the Lamb who was slain (5:12).

The *Didache*, after providing Matthew's text of the 'Our Father', immediately directs Christians to recite it three times a day, a direction which will turn up in the fourth-century *Apostolic Constitutions* (7:24). Apparently the *Didache* is referring to the three hours of prayer, which Jews had practised (Dan. 6:10; Ps. 55:17) and Christians had continued to practise (Acts 2:15; 3:1; 10:3, 9). Clearly by the start of the second century the Lord's Prayer was understood to be central to Christian life – a centrality also suggested by the way in which the *Didache* recalls the prayer between its teaching on baptism and the Eucharist and so implies that it is an essential part of the believers' worship and witness.

The *Didache* signals the 'triumph' of Matthew's version of the 'Our Father' over the shorter Lucan version, which can be translated as follows:

> Father, may your name be made holy.
> May your kingdom come.
> Give us each day our daily bread.
> And forgive us our sins,
> as we ourselves forgive everyone in debt to us.
> And do not bring us into temptation. (Luke 11:2–4)

From the time of Origen in the second century, Christian writers have reflected on the existence of two, differing versions of the Lord's Prayer. Origen himself accounted for the two versions by proposing that on two separate occasions Jesus himself provided a longer and a shorter text for prayer.[2] Even though they cannot rule out this possible explanation, most scholars nowadays seek an explanation in terms of the evangelists themselves and their different communities. In the course of this book we will see characteristics of Matthew and plausible reasons for him and/or others adding to the text from Jesus and producing the longer version. Luke's hand can be spotted in two variants. By adding 'each day (*kath' hēmeran*)' to what seems the original saying from Jesus about 'taking up one's cross' (Mark 8:34), Luke has already underlined the day-by-day slog involved in being a disciple. (Luke 9:23). One can easily see him turning a simple 'today (*sēmeron*)' into 'each day' or 'day by day (*kath' hēmeran*)'. Second, for readers who would not understand 'debts' to be an Aramaic euphemism for 'sins', Luke replaces the original language of 'forgive us our debts (*opheilēmata*)' with 'forgive us our sins (*hamartias*)'.[3]

But in appreciating fully the Lord's Prayer, the setting provided by Luke is significant. The disciples have observed Jesus at prayer. When he stops, they immediately ask him to help them also to pray (Luke 11:1–2). They want to pray like him and bond with him in prayer. The Lucan setting shows us that in praying the 'Our Father' we pray not only as Jesus taught us but also (in part) like Jesus himself.[4] As we shall see, the 'Our Father' sums up in prayer much of what Jesus did and taught. We are fully justified in praying it 'with Jesus' and consciously feeling in our prayer his intentions, words and actions.[5]

Without forgetting the Lucan version, this book will reflect phrase by phrase and word by word on what we have from Matthew. But before doing so, it is well worth remembering the numerous ways in which for almost two thousand years Christians have (both publicly and privately) prayed, interpreted and lived the Lord's Prayer. Beyond question, we need to scrutinise its origins and meaning as we have it from Matthew and Luke. But we would neglect at our peril the endlessly rich impact it has enjoyed for almost two millennia. German scholarship introduced the helpful theme of the *Wirkungsgeschichte* (history of effect or impact). Along with some other NT texts, the Lord's Prayer has triggered an amazingly rich history of usage in the public and private life of Christians. Hence, while it is vital to ask what the prayer meant to Jesus himself, his first followers and two gospel writers, we must also recall what the 'Our Father' has continued to mean over the centuries and what it means today. Neither here nor elsewhere should we tolerate any wedge between what Jesus (or the gospel writers) taught and intended and what Christians in any age have understood when, in their many different languages, they pray the Lord's Prayer.

Christians have consistently preached and written about the Lord's Prayer over the centuries. The oldest extant commentary on it comes from Tertullian, who died around 220. Origen, who was one of the greatest biblical theologians of all time and died around 254, dedicated a long section of his *Treatise on Prayer* to the 'Our Father'. St Cyprian of Carthage (d. 258), when commenting on the 'Our Father', was the first to refer to it as the 'Lord's Prayer (*oratio domenica*)'. The immense amount of literature on the Lord's Prayer witnesses to the way it has been treasured by Christians of all ages.

A building which stands to the east of Jerusalem on the Mount of Olives, the Church of the Pater Noster (Our Father), vividly attests the universal devotion to the Lord's Prayer. The Emperor Constantine, soon after he gave religious freedom to Christians in 313, began a building programme in Palestine focused around three caves: the cave of Jesus' birth in Bethlehem, the tomb cut out of rock near Golgotha, and a cave on the Mount of Olives which tradition linked with Jesus' teaching and ascension. Over this cave a church was built under the direction of Constantine's mother, St Helena; a raised sanctuary covered the cave. Persians destroyed this church in 614; five centuries later the Crusaders erected an oratory in the ruins. By that time, the cave and the site had become exclusively associated with the teaching of Jesus and, in particular, with his teaching the 'Our Father'. After the foundations of Helena's church were uncovered in the early twentieth century, the present Church of the Pater Noster was built on the same site. Tiled panels in the church and the adjacent cloister were decorated with the Lord's Prayer in 62 languages. Up to the year 2000, other versions of the Lord's Prayer were added and one can now read the prayer in at least one hundred versions. Like the story of his birth, death and resurrection, the prayer Jesus shared with his disciples has gone out to all nations and cultures.

In this book we will move from the three 'you' petitions, or prayers for divine action, to the four 'we' petitions, or requests which express the essential needs of the disciples of Jesus. Many notable Christians (e.g. St Augustine of Hippo, Martin Luther and Lancelot Andrewes) have distinguished seven petitions. Some (e.g. St Maximus the Confessor, John Calvin and Jeremy Taylor) have drawn together the petitions about temptation and evil, and interpreted the Lord's Prayer as sixfold. But my aim is not to adjudicate such matters but rather to help readers understand, treasure and pray with greater insight and devotion the 'Our Father'. I am most grateful to Stephen Pisano and to several readers of this manuscript for different kinds of help. The scholarly insights of Dr Kenneth Stevenson, Anglican Bishop of Portsmouth, have guided some of what follows. I dedicate this book to Mary Wilsey and Maggie Mason, who founded *Wanted in Rome* and have been such great friends to generations of Romans.

Gerald O'Collins SJ
Gregorian University, Rome

◆
ABBREVIATIONS

NT New Testament
OT Old Testament
par(r). and parallel(s) in other gospel(s)

Part 1

◆

ADDRESSING GOD

♦

Chapter 1

STARTING WITH 'ABBA'

> One is justified in claiming that Jesus' striking use of *Abba*
> did express his intimate experience of God as his own
> father and that this usage did make a lasting impression
> on his disciples.
>
> John P. Meier, *The New Jerome Biblical Commentary*

> With the sweetly melodious harp of your divine heart,
> through the power of the Holy Spirit, the Paraclete, I sing
> to you, Lord God, adorable Father, songs of praise and
> thanksgiving on behalf of all creatures in heaven, on
> earth and under the earth; all which are, were and shall
> be.
>
> St Gertrude of Helfta, *The Herald of Divine Love*

THE LORD'S PRAYER IS intriguingly simple but almost
overpoweringly rich. This holds true right from the very
first word in the versions from both Matthew and Luke: 'Patēr
(Father)', the Greek rendering of what Jesus said in his mother
tongue (Aramaic), 'Abba'. In Matthew's version, 'of us
(hēmōn)' follows 'Father' at once. The classical Latin translation of Matthew's version ('Pater noster') and translations into
some modern languages can maintain the order of the original
Greek: for instance, in German ('Vater unser'), Italian ('Padre
nostro') and Spanish ('Padre nuestro'). Let me keep to the

order of Matthew and begin with a word which encourages a new and familiar way of relating to God: 'Father'. Speaking that way to God embodies a new 'freedom of access' and a 'confidence born of trust' (Eph. 3:12) which Jesus preached and practised. He made it the favoured name through which his followers addressed and spoke of God. The very first word of the 'Our Father' is decisive. Jesus directed his disciples to pray to God primarily as 'Abba' and not as 'King of the universe' or 'Lord of heaven and earth'.

The rhetorical, theological and autobiographical style of St Paul's letters set him apart from the story-telling form of Jesus' preaching, with its mixture of parables and concise maxims. Where Jesus in a straightforward way taught his hearers, 'ask and you shall receive, seek and you shall find' (Matt. 7:7), the apostle presented the Holy Spirit as a kind of personal tutor who comes to the aid of human weakness. He told the Christians of Rome: 'We do not even know how we ought to pray, but through our inarticulate groans the Spirit himself is pleading for us' (Rom. 8:26). Nevertheless, in the greetings with which he opened his letters, Paul preserved the distinctive usage of Jesus: 'Grace and peace to you from God *our Father* and the Lord Jesus Christ' (e.g. Rom. 1:7). Writing to the Christian communities in Rome and Galatia (that is to say, beyond the area of Aramaic speakers), Paul also recognised that they too, through their new life of faith and grace, spoke to God with the very word used by Jesus: 'The Spirit enables you to cry "Abba! Father"' (Rom. 8:15). In an earlier letter Paul insisted on the interior work of the Spirit in making that prayer possible: 'God has sent into our hearts the Spirit of his Son, crying "Abba! Father"' (Gal. 4:6). A straight line led from the teaching of Jesus on God as Father to Christians around the Mediterranean world praying to God as 'Abba'. Paul understands *the* gift of the final age of salvation to be the new relationship with God expressed by 'Abba', a relationship which the Holy Spirit makes possible and expresses.

Some have argued that by naming God 'Father', Jesus and

4

then his followers have underwritten the oppression of women and helped to maintain a patriarchal system in society and the Church. Before addressing this issue directly, let me examine the roots for this distinctive name, which, especially through the 'Our Father', has left its central mark on the belief, worship and life of Christians.

When we reflect on what Jesus meant by 'God', we need to recall three sources for the images and language he used: (1) the Jewish scriptures he inherited; (2) his own experience of growing up in rural Galilee; and (3) his own life of deep prayer. (1) One can presume that he heard, read and prayed over the Jewish scriptures frequently and lovingly. Jesus was imbued with what we call the Jewish scriptures. (2) The gospels, especially those by Matthew, Mark and Luke, show us how Jesus took in very attentively the world around him and drew many of his characteristic images from that source. If we put together the images and language these gospels record, we have rich insights into the life of ancient Galilee. (3) The gospels also remember Jesus' deep life of prayer; they recall him giving generous and constant time to prayer. But unlike St Teresa of Avila and other great mystics, he never put down in writing his experience of God in prayer. There are hints of what happened to Jesus in prayer: for example, in the Garden of Gethsemane. For the most part, however, we have only occasional hints and glimpses. We can at least say this: in his constant prayer, Jesus looked into the mystery of God and he called that mystery 'Father'; he experienced the divine mystery as 'Abba'. Yet we are on firmer ground if we concentrate on the first two sources. Let us look first at the biblical roots for Jesus' distinctive language about God.

'FATHER' IN THE JEWISH SCRIPTURES

Before recalling the (rather scarce) OT use of 'Father' language for God, we should note that even if the OT neither directly speaks of nor addresses God as anyone's 'Mother', it does use maternal similes in this context. God is graphically compared with a woman who suffers in childbirth (Isa. 42:14), as well as with a midwife (Ps. 22:9–10). Comparisons with maternal conception and begetting are also pressed into service elsewhere (Num. 11:12; Deut. 32:18). As a mother does, God wishes to comfort the suffering people (Isa. 66:13). The divine love even exceeds that of a woman for her children: 'Can a woman forget the nursing child, or show no compassion for the child of her womb? Even these may forget, yet I will not forget you' (Isa. 49:15). A tenderness beyond that of a mother is highlighted by Sirach: 'The Most High will be more tender to you than a mother' (4:10).

At the outset it is worth recalling how simile differs from metaphor.[1] A simile uses language in its *customary sense* to compare an aspect of something or someone with that of something or someone else. In the case of Isaiah 42:14, God's 'loud' intervention is likened to a woman gasping and panting in labour. Metaphor *extends* the use of language beyond its 'ordinary' meaning(s) to generate new perspectives on reality by asserting an identity between two subjects (and not by merely comparing two aspects): for instance, 'God is Father to the people.' This statement contains some crucial information about God that emerges in the OT, and then is hugely developed by Jesus and his followers.

In the OT scriptures, God is known by many names, above all through the personal name of YHWH (e.g. Exod. 3:14; 6:6–8), the most sacred of names that is used about 6,800 times in the OT, both by itself or in compounds like YHWH *Malak* ('King'; e.g. Ps. 93:1). God is also known as *El* ('divinity'): as in *El Shaddai*, 'God the One of the Mountain(s)' (e.g. Exod. 6:3; Num. 24:4, 16), the intensified plural *Elohim* ('divine God'), and *El Elyon* ('God most High'). Marc Zvi Brettler has pointed out that 'God is King' is the predominant metaphor for God in the OT, appearing much more frequently than metaphors such as 'God is a lover/husband' or 'God is a father'.[2] But what do we find about the last metaphor, the one that particularly interests us in connection with the opening of the Lord's Prayer? A little more than twenty times God is named (or addressed) as 'Father' in the OT. Let us look first at the cases in the proto-canonical books (those thirty-nine books accepted by all Christians as inspired and canonical) and then at those in the (later) deuterocanonical books (or the six books and further portions of the proto-canonical books found in the Greek but not in the Hebrew canon of the scriptures).

'Father' in the proto-canonical books

One of the oldest texts in which God is called 'Father' comes from a song attributed to Moses: 'Do you thus repay the Lord, O foolish and senseless people? Is he not your Father, who formed you, who made you and established you?' (Deut. 32:6). Moses is pictured as recalling the intimate covenant bond between God and the people. By flirting with other religions, the people deny their true parentage and behave like ungrateful children. God's nurturing fidelity and mercy are contrasted with the perverse infidelity of Israel. This text from Deuteronomy indicates how 'Father', when used of God, usually refers to the special relationship between God and the people who have been delivered from captivity and called God's son (e.g. Exod. 4:22–23; Hos. 11:1) or God's 'sons and daughters' (e.g. Deut. 32:19; Isa. 1:2; 30:1). God gave them birth by electing and adopting them. An historical divine choice, and not any kind of sexual activity and physical generation (as in the case of gendered gods of surrounding nations), made God their 'Father'.

A later passage recalls God's promise to King David: 'I will raise up your offspring after you ... and will establish the throne of his kingdom forever. I will be a father to him, and he shall be a son to me' (2 Sam. 7:12–14). In the ancient Middle East rulers were styled 'sons of God'. Hence it is not surprising to find God's promise about an everlasting Davidic dynasty mentioning Solomon, David's son and successor, in these terms. The royal psalms reflected the belief that the anointed king was divinely chosen and was deemed to be God's adopted son: 'You are my son; today I have begotten you' (Ps. 2:7). The psalm refers to the day when the king was installed as the people's God-given leader.

The king was understood to rule by divine choice, through God's power, and in fulfilment of God's purpose. Being enthroned on Mount Zion where God was believed to 'dwell' (Ps. 2:6), the royal son of David was legitimated by God his 'Father' – God's son in that sense but not in the sense of physical sonship (as if he were literally God's offspring), nor in the sense of being divinised or literally made divine. By naming God as 'Father', the oracle delivered in 2 Samuel 7 brings out the unconditional nature of the promise and rela-tionship. No matter what happens, God's choice of the Davidic dynasty, like the divine election of the whole people, has established a permanent relationship: God is and will remain the faithful 'Father' to the people and its king.

The Psalms yield two passages that speak directly, and more passages that speak indirectly (as in Psalm 2), of the divine fatherhood. Psalm 68 praises the God of heaven who is named as 'Father' to the defenceless:

> Sing of God, sing praises to his name;
> lift up a song to him who rides upon the clouds –
> his name is the Lord –
> Be exultant before him.
> *Father* of orphans and protector of widows
> is God in his holy habitation.
> God gives the desolate a home to live in;
> He leads out the prisoners to prosperity,
> but the rebellious live in a parched land. (Ps. 68:4–6)

The God whose strength is expressed by the standard image of 'riding upon the clouds' places his power at the service of the powerless, the forsaken and the imprisoned. God acts as 'Father' toward them all.

A royal psalm for deliverance, Psalm 89 is unusual in that someone (here the king) addresses God as 'Father', even though the address is placed by God in the mouth of the king.[3] God speaks of his 'faithful one' (David):

> He shall cry to me, 'You are my *Father*,
> My God, and the Rock of my salvation!'
> I will make him the first-born,
> the highest of the kings of the earth.
> Forever I will keep my steadfast love for him,
> and my covenant with him will stand firm.
> I will establish his line forever. (Ps. 89:26–29)

The Davidic king will address God as 'Father', the God whose strong fidelity to his covenanted love entitles God to be also named as 'Rock of salvation'.

Turning to the prophetic literature, we can start with Jeremiah and oracular material from the late seventh century, when Judah was threatened by both external forces and internal infidelity. In the first passage God is presented as both 'Father' and 'Bridegroom' (or 'Friend'), in the second as 'Father' to his children; in both passages the people are encouraged to address God as 'my Father'. In the first passage God exhorts the people to repent of their infidelity: 'Have you not just now called to me, "My Father; you are the Friend (or Bridegroom) of my youth – will he be angry forever, will he be indignant to the end?" This is how you have spoken, but you have done all the evil that you could' (Jer. 3:4–5). In the second passage, God explains how Judah's infidelity has blocked the divine hope that the people will call God 'My Father': 'I thought how I would set you among my children, and give you a pleasant land, the most beautiful heritage of all the nations. And I thought you would call me *My Father*, and would not turn from following me' (Jer. 3:19).

A sharp contrast comes through these two passages. God follows his children with a father's love and fidelity, but they fall into infidelity and indulge idolatrous attitudes, even saying to a tree, 'You are my father' (Jer. 2:27). God does not bear grudges against the people but expects a loyal love that will not only address him as 'My Father' but also act accordingly. The first passage interweaves the imagery of father and lover; paternal and marital love express the partnership that God maintains with the people. The latter image, with God as 'Husband' to the people, recurs in prophetic literature (e.g. Isa. 54:4–8; Jer. 2:2; Ezek. 16:1–63; Hos. 2:7, 19) and probably helped to keep talk of YHWH as 'Father' to a minimum. Another obvious reason why the OT rarely applied to God the metaphor of 'Father' was that such usage could have suggested the 'natural', procreative activity attributed to Baal, Asherah and other gods and goddesses of the Near East. Far from being that kind of biological or physical parent, YHWH had no consort. The divine fatherhood (and the Israelites' corresponding status as God's sons and daughters) was understood, as we have seen, to result from the free divine choice and activity in the history of salvation.

The closing chapters of Isaiah yield two further examples for our study of the background to Jesus' distinctive usage. At least some of the exiles have returned from Babylon to Jerusalem, when the prophet voices the community's laments in one of the very few passages in which God is addressed as 'Father' and, in fact, is identified and addressed as 'our Father': 'For you are *our Father*, though Abraham does not know us and Israel does not acknowledge us; you, O Lord, are *our Father*; our Redeemer from of old is your name' (Isa. 63:16). The patriarchs, Abraham and Israel (i.e. Jacob), have died and are of no help. God, the people's Redeemer from of old, is immortal and as 'our Father' revives hopes for salvation. In a prayer that God will reveal himself and act again with power, the prophet confesses not only the people's sin and helplessness but also their trust in the Father who has made them: 'You have hidden your face from us, and have delivered us up to our iniquity. Yet, O Lord, you are *our Father*; we the clay, you the potter; we are all the work of your hands' (Isa. 64:6–8). The Book of Isaiah began by calling God 'our God' (Isa. 1:10); it ends by addressing YHWH as 'our Father', the people's God who will care for them in their distress and patiently mold them as a potter does with clay.

'Father' in the deuterocanonical books

Turning to the deuterocanonical books (books found in the Greek but not the Hebrew canon of scripture), we begin with a hymn of praise that comes at the end of Tobit: 'Exalt him [God] in the presence of every living being, because he is our Lord and he is our God; he is *our Father* and he is God forever' (Tob. 13:4). This prayer of praise discloses a very personal attitude towards God that recalls what we have just seen from Isaiah 64 and anticipates the prayerful relationship to God 'our Father', so characteristic of Jesus and his followers. The Book of Tobit is a piece of edifying and fascinating fiction, whose main protagonists (Tobit, his son Tobias and Sarah, the bride-to-be) offer vivid examples of tenacious faith when tested by painful and even terrifying challenges. The hymn that praises God as 'our Father' and 'our God' may have been added later. At all events the book and its concluding hymn show God's loving, paternal concern for Tobit, his family and all those who suffer in exile.

In denouncing those who trust idols to bring them and their ships safely across the sea, the Book of Wisdom turns to God and confesses: 'It is your providence, *O Father*, that steers its [the ship's] course, because you have given it a path in the sea and a safe way through the waves' (Wisd. 14:3). God's fatherly providence powerfully controls ships, seas, and all creation. Earlier, Wisdom's account of the false way, enter- tained and followed by ungodly persons, includes their plans to torture and even kill the righteous person, who 'boasts that God is *his father*' (Wisd. 2:16).

11

SIMILES AND COROLLARIES

To complete this summary account of 'Father' language for God in the OT, we need to recall the use of similes, some corollaries and then some data from intertestamental literature. First of all, a few passages compared God's activity toward the people with that of an ideal father. In the wilderness, God marvellously 'carried' the people to their destination 'as a father carries his son' (Deut. 1:31). Yet such paternal similes for God were quite rare, just as the metaphor of 'Father' for God was also rare in the OT.

The OT used more frequently the corollary of fatherhood by speaking of God's sons, daughters or children. Israel had become God's 'son' (e.g. Hos. 11:1) or 'firstborn son' (e.g. Exod. 4:22). Although a sense of collective sonship predominated in pre-Christian Judaism, royal and righteous persons were also at times singled out. As we have seen, the king was also named God's 'son' and so too was a righteous person. But it was above all the people as a whole who, through the divine choice and liberating activity, enjoyed the status of God's 'sons', 'sons and daughters' or 'children'. This language expressed the intimate closeness of Israel's relationship to God, and nowhere more clearly than in Hosea 11:1–4.

While Hosea elsewhere uses the metaphor of God as 'Husband' to the people, here he introduces the tender metaphor of loving parents patiently bringing up their children. This involves teaching the children to walk (by using a kind of harness), hugging them, kissing them and feeding them. The prophet portrays God's gentle, parental activity as follows: 'It is I who taught Ephraim to walk, I took them in my arms. But they did not know that I secured them with reins and led them with bonds of love, that I lifted them like a little child to my cheek, that I bent down to feed them' (Hos. 11:3–4). No passage in the OT goes beyond this one in expressing God's tender care for his rebellious children. Where the law allowed a rebellious son to be brought by his parents to the elders and then stoned to death (Deut. 21:18–21), God's parental love will not surrender the people to their sinful choices. God is the most loving of parents, even when faced with children who are consistently unloving and unresponsive.

The intertestamental literature (texts composed by Jews around the time of Jesus but not recognised as canonical scripture) includes a few examples of paternal and maternal language for God. There is a tender passage from the Thanksgiving Hymns of Qumran. It applies to God a metaphor ('Thou art a father') and two similes ('as a woman' and 'as a foster-father'): 'For Thou art a father to all [the sons] of Thy truth, and as a woman who tenderly loves her babe, so dost Thou rejoice in them; and as a foster-father bearing a child in his lap, so carest Thou for all thy creatures.'[4] One should add, however, that in the very few places where the Dead Sea Scrolls introduce the theme of divine fatherhood and the filial status of human beings (e.g. 4Q372.1.16), the relationship remains unrelated to God's 'Spirit'. As we saw above, Jesus *and his Spirit* enter the picture when Paul refers to believers being adopted as God's sons and daughters.

To sum up the (limited) biblical background to the 'Abba-talk' of Jesus: naming God 'Father' expressed the divine involvement in the story of Israel, its kingly leaders and its righteous ones. The 'Father' metaphor centred, above all, on the free, divine choice of a people, whom God has delivered from Egypt and steadfastly cherished. Despite their sinful failures, the people could always experience God as their 'Father'. Nevertheless, while occurring in some historical, prophetic and sapiential texts, this divine name was not frequent in the OT. It hardly ever occurred in prayers addressed to God. Jesus changed that, influenced more (as we shall see in the next chapter) by his experience of daily life around him than by his Jewish heritage. Before we come to his experience, we must sketch his usage.

JESUS AND 'ABBA'

The Gospel of Mark several times calls God 'Father' (in Greek, *patēr*), most strikingly in Jesus' prayer in Gethsemane: 'Abba, Father, all things are possible to you; take this cup from me. Yet not my will but yours be done' (Mark 14:36). In the mother tongue of Jesus, 'Abba' was the way children and grown-ups addressed their male parent as 'my own dear father'. It was rather like the situation in modern Italian where grown-ups continue to speak to their male parent as they did when they were children: 'babbo (daddy)'. Jesus evidently spoke of and with God as his 'Abba', in a direct and familial manner that seems to have been unknown, or at least highly unusual, in the earlier Jewish tradition in Palestine. 'Abba' was remembered as a characteristic and distinctive feature of Jesus' prayer life.[5] It reproduced the unaffected attitude of children who totally trust their loving father; it introduced the Lord's Prayer in which direct and short petitions mirror a childlike dependence on an all-powerful and loving father in whom one can have unconditional confidence.

In several passages in Matthew (e.g. 6:9; 11:25–26; 16:17), in at least one passage in Luke (11:2), and perhaps in other passages of those two gospels, 'Father (*patēr*)' stands for the original 'Abba'.[6] The example of Jesus, at least in the early days of Christianity, encouraged his followers to address God in prayer with the familiar 'Abba' (Gal. 4:6; Rom. 8:15). As J. D. G. Dunn points out, 'the clear implication' of these two passages is that Paul regarded the 'Abba' prayer 'as something distinctive to those who had received the eschatological Spirit' – in other words, 'as a distinguishing mark of those who shared the Spirit of Jesus' sonship, of an inheritance shared with Christ'.[7]

Altogether in the synoptic gospels (excluding simply parallel cases), Jesus speaks of 'Father', 'my (heavenly) Father', 'your (heavenly) Father' or 'our Father' 51 times. Sometimes we deal with a Father-saying which has been drawn from Q, or a source ('Quelle' in German) containing sayings of Jesus used by Matthew and Luke (e.g. Matt. 11:25–27; parallel in Luke 10:21–22), or else we find a Father-saying which, while attested by Matthew alone (e.g. Matt. 16:17) or by Luke alone (e.g. Luke 22:29), seems to go back to Jesus himself. Matthew shows a liking for 'heavenly' and at various points may have added the adjective to sayings that originally spoke only of 'your Father' or 'my Father' (e.g. Matt. 6:32). The same evangelist may at times have also inserted 'Father' into his sources (e.g. Matt. 12:50; 20:23; 26:29). Even 'discounting' a number of examples as created by the evangelists themselves or by the traditions they drew on, it is clear that Jesus spoke fairly frequently of God as 'Abba (Father dear)'. In perhaps the most important of these instances, Jesus referred to the Father, identified as 'Lord of heaven and earth', and claimed that a unique and exclusive knowledge of 'the Father' was possessed by 'the Son', who was tacitly identified as 'me': 'All things have been delivered to me by my Father; and no one knows the Son except the Father, and no one knows the Father except the Son and anyone to whom the Son chooses to reveal him' (Matt. 11:27; parallel in Luke 10:22).[8] This was to affirm a unique mutual knowledge and relationship of Jesus as the Son to the Father, a mutual relationship out of which Jesus revealed, not a previously unknown God, but the God whom he alone knew fully and really.

Further, Jesus called those who did God's will 'my brother, and sister, and mother', but not 'my father' (Mark 3:31–35). He invited his hearers to accept God as their loving, merciful Father. He worked toward mediating to them a new relationship with God, even to the point that they too could use 'Abba' when addressing God in prayer. However, being his brothers and sisters did not put them on the same level with him as sons and daughters of God. Jesus apparently distinguished between 'my' Father and 'your' Father, a distinction upheld by Matthew. He did not invite his disciples to share with him an *identical* relationship of sonship. No saying has been preserved in which Jesus linked the disciples with himself so that *together* they could say, 'Our Father'. When he encouraged the disciples to pray to God as Father, the word 'our' in 'Our Father' (Matt. 6:9, unlike Luke 11:2 which has no 'our') was for the disciples only.[9] Even if Jesus did actually say 'Our Father', it was in a prayer he was understood to propose for others ('pray then like this' – Matt. 6:9). He invited his hearers to accept a new relationship with God as Father; yet it was a relationship that depended on his relationship with God (Luke 22:29–30) and differed from it. When Jesus spoke of 'my Father', was he conscious of being 'Son' in some kind of distinctive way? Or was he even aware of a unique sonship vis-à-vis 'Abba'?

At least we can say this: Jesus applied the language of divine sonship individually (to himself), filling it with a meaning that lifted 'Son (of God)' beyond the level of his *merely* being a man made like Adam in the divine image (Luke 3:38), or someone perfectly sensitive to the Holy Spirit (Luke 4:1, 14, 18), or someone bringing God's peace (Luke 2:14; 10:5–6) albeit in his own way (Matt. 10:34; parallel in Luke 12:51), or even a/the Davidic king (Luke 1:33) who would in some way restore the kingdom of Israel. We do not have to argue simply from the fact that Jesus referred to himself as 'the Son' (Mark 12:1–12; 13:32; Matt. 11:27) and to God as 'my Father'. He not only spoke 'like the Son' but also acted 'like the Son' in knowing and revealing the truth about God, in changing the divine law, in forgiving sins (outside the normal channels of temple sacrifice and the ministry of the levitical priesthood), in being the one through whom others could become children of God, and in acting with total obedience as *the* agent for God's final kingdom. All this clarifies the charge of blasphemy brought against him at the end (Mark 14:64); he had given the impression of standing on a par with God. Jesus had come across as expressing a unique filial consciousness and as laying claim to a unique filial relationship with the God whom in a startling way he addressed as 'Abba'.

Even if historically he never called himself *the only Son of God* (see John 1:14, 18; 3:16, 18), Jesus presented himself as *Son* (upper case) and not just as one who was the divinely appointed Messiah and in that sense *son* (lower case) of God.[10] He made himself out to be more than just someone chosen and anointed as divine representative to fulfil a final role in and for the kingdom of God. Implicitly Jesus claimed a personal relationship of sonship towards God that provided the grounds for his functions as revealer, lawgiver, forgiver of sins, and agent of the final kingdom. Those functions (his 'doing') depended on his unique, personal relationship to 'Abba' inasmuch as he was Son of God (his 'being').

Since Jesus experienced and expressed himself as the Son, that means that the God of the OT was now known to be the Father. As Tertullian appreciated in his exposition of the Lord's Prayer, the revelation of *the* Son was necessarily implied in the revelation of the Father, and vice versa.[11]

'FATHER' TODAY

Recalling how Jesus gave himself totally to proclaiming the kingdom of God, many have called the Lord's Prayer the prayer of the kingdom, the prayer which summarises the entire message of the kingdom. Its very first word, 'Abba (Father)', sets the tone and is the heart of the matter. In proclaiming the kingdom, Jesus announced a loving, merciful Father, the God with whom we can enjoy a truly intimate and privileged relationship. It is this relationship to God the Father which makes the disciples of Jesus who they are. They find in 'Abba' the very source of their own existence. They are protected and empowered by 'Abba' to be really and authentically themselves. The various petitions in the Lord's Prayer will help them move ahead in this relationship.

The followers of Jesus formalise their discipleship through

the sacrament of baptism which expresses their basic faith in the Father, the Son and the Holy Spirit. These are the names on which leading voices of Christianity have insisted from the beginning. In the fourth century St Basil of Caesarea (d. 379) wrote with assurance: 'We are bound to be baptised in the terms we have received and to profess faith in the terms in which we have been baptised, and as we have professed faith in, so to give glory to the Father, Son, and Holy Spirit' (*Epistle*, 125.3). Basil's older contemporary, St Athanasius of Alexandria (d. 373), systematically examined the fatherhood of God, as well as reflecting at length on the Holy Spirit. Fatherhood, he insisted, belongs eternally to God and defines the being of God. In other words, the Father–Son relationship necessarily enters into the Christian definition of the word 'God',[12] as it does into the opening word of the Lord's Prayer.

Nowadays, at least in some countries, pressure for inclusive God-language questions what Athanasius championed and what the Lord's Prayer proposes. How much of a future should the gender-specific name of 'Father' enjoy? Has the language of divine fatherhood, by fostering a male-related image of God, legitimated male domination, underpinned the power structure of patriarchal Christianity, and proved a major cause of women being oppressed in the Western world and beyond? Does naming God 'Father' presuppose an anti-woman orientation and encourage chauvinist attitudes? Should we happily envisage remodelling the Lord's Prayer and open by addressing 'our Creator', 'our Parent', or 'our Father-Mother'? Or will reflection on the experience and teaching of Jesus suggest otherwise?

Chapter 2

♦

SAVING 'ABBA'

Nowadays some christians find speech about God as 'Father' problematic. Every human father we know is imperfect, some of them dreadfully so. As Peter Steele remarked in a homily preached at Newman College (University of Melbourne) in August 2001, 'a taint of that imperfection can attach itself to any father-talk'. What then is to be said about the 'father-talk' with which the Lord's Prayer begins? What kind of 'Father' did Jesus have in mind? Was Jesus proposing a motherly-fatherly 'Abba'?

At that time 'Abba' was used of one's male parent, but never used for God in Jewish liturgical prayer or as an address to God in one's personal prayer. Hence we need to look at the preaching through which Jesus filled out what 'Abba' meant for him and how he experienced God. Those who see in Jesus the mirror image on earth of 'Abba' can also have some sense of what God is like by looking at the way Jesus himself behaved.

THE WITNESS OF JESUS TO ABBA

Jesus taught his followers to address God as 'Abba', and that raises the question: what kind of fathers did Jesus see and meet? What kind of men did he experience when growing up?

19

From his preaching it is obvious that he saw farmers sowing seeds and reaping crops, owners of flocks caring for sheep and cattle, fishermen catching fish and mending nets, and owners of vineyards hiring extra workers at the time of harvest. Presumably most of these men were married and had children. Their activities at times illustrated for Jesus something of the heavenly Father he cherished. Shepherds could go to a great deal of trouble to find the one sheep who had strayed from a flock of a hundred (Luke 15:4–7; parallel in Matt. 18:12–14). The owner of a vineyard, perhaps at the time of harvest, might be exceptionally generous with those who had joined his team of workers only late in the afternoon (Matt. 20:1–16). We can presume that Joseph, the husband of Mary, led the mind and heart of Jesus in the direction of 'Abba'. But, apart from a few verses at the start of Matthew's gospel, we know tantalisingly little about Joseph and his impact on Jesus. Works by such artists as Sir Edward Burne-Jones (d. 1898), Caravaggio (d. 1610) and other artists may encourage us to imagine something of the ways in which as a child and boy Jesus experienced Joseph.

Out of his experience and prayer, Jesus was to teach his followers to address God as 'Abba'. But he did not depict God in terms that would have been associated exclusively with male activities of his time. He encouraged his disciples to think of God as also being like a woman coping with a minor emergency such as searching for her lost property (Luke 15:8–10), or doing ordinary things such as adding a little yeast when baking bread (Luke 13:20–21; parallel in Matt. 13:33). Jesus found nothing in the scriptures that could have given rise to his parables of the lost coin and the hidden yeast. Apropos of the latter, St Paul was to follow the OT scriptures when he associated yeast with 'malice and evil' (1 Cor. 5:8). But not Jesus, in one of his parables that came out of his experience of women doing various things.

Jesus could easily have heard of a woman, perhaps someone who lived nearby, who lost a tiny silver coin, found it after searching carefully, and then shared her joy with her friends and neighbours. Jesus himself might have been one of those neighbours. It seems that we hear from him a story that came right out of what he had experienced. Certainly in the case of the hidden yeast, from childhood on he enjoyed innumerable chances of seeing his mother and other women doing just what he said: mixing the right amount of yeast in the flour they were kneading for the oven. When he saw women at that kitchen task, his mind moved ever so easily to God. Years later in his preaching he wanted to share with others his experience of God being and acting like women doing such things.

Those two parables work very well. The first, that of the lost coin, comes in a chapter (15:3–32) where Luke brings together three parables of loss. One of those parables, the story of the prodigal son, portrays someone who has been lost morally and religiously. But he is still able to make his own way home. Then there is the lost sheep. It has little chance of finding its way back through the wilderness to the shepherd and the other ninety-nine sheep. Yet that could happen; a frightened and dim-witted sheep just might stumble on the right path. But a coin lost in a dusty corner of a badly lit house cannot do anything itself so as to be found again. It pictures perfectly the helplessness of lost human beings who must wait to be found again. But they will be found. God will seek them out with the diligence and concern of a woman who has lost something valuable.

In his childhood Jesus watched his mother at work and saw for himself the power of a little yeast to affect a whole lump of dough. What came from adding the yeast followed with certainty: the flour rose, and a large, fragrant loaf was ready for the table. That elementary domestic experience involving a woman entered the way Jesus thought about God and the growth of the divine kingdom. The divine power may be hidden but it will certainly leaven everything. Immense and wonderful results are sure to come; we will eat bread together in the future kingdom of God. This parable of the hidden yeast not only speaks of the power of God but also hints at the loving care of a mother who prepares bread for her hungry family.

In this and other ways, the teaching of Jesus filled out what he meant by 'Abba'. The two parables suggest that a womanly perspective on God also belonged to what he meant. It comes as no surprise then that, although 'King' was a frequent title for God in the OT and in the Judaism of his time and although Jesus himself constantly proclaimed the kingdom of God, he referred only once to God as 'King'. He called Jerusalem 'the city of the great King' (Matt. 5:35) – a solitary example that derives from the teaching of Jesus against the necessity of oaths.[1] To be sure, 'King' could be understood with a range of ideal characteristics (e.g. Isa. 11:1–9), but Jesus avoided speaking of God as 'King'.

Jesus talked rather of 'Abba' and the astounding readiness to forgive sinners which characterised this fatherly-motherly God (e.g. Matt. 6:14; Mark 11:25). Jesus wanted to share his new vision of the world and, in particular, of the fresh possibilities God offers us. Jesus' stories cherish the powerful and loving way God deals with us. The parable of the prodigal son, which would be better called the parable of the merciful father (Luke 15:11–32), is the longest story Jesus left in answer to the questions: What is 'Abba' like? What is he doing for us? The parable never introduces 'love' either as a noun or a verb. But it is unintelligible unless we think of the divine and human love revealed by Jesus. Without mentioning this parable, the First Letter of John sums up what it is about: 'God is love' (1 John 4:8, 16). Love, above all merciful love, is the most fundamental feature of God. In the parable of the prodigal son Jesus told a story that takes place over and over again when dissatisfied young men and women want to break with their families and indulge their freedom. But Jesus gave the story an unusual twist. All too often when prodigals return home, they may not find much love. They will hardly ever find the astonishingly merciful and unconditional love with which the father of the prodigal son treats his sinful child. This story runs counter to what we might expect to happen when such a young rascal trudges home.

The story also ran counter to what those who first heard this parable must have expected. They were used to the biblical stories of two or more brothers, in which the younger one wins out over the older brother (or brothers). That was what happened in the Book of Genesis when the younger Jacob succeeded in getting the inheritance in place of Esau (Gen. 27:1–45), Jacob won and Esau lost. Something similar occurred when Joseph triumphed over his older brothers. His father (Jacob) loved Joseph 'more than any other of his children, because he was the son of his old age' (Gen. 37:3). Unlike the prodigal son, Joseph did not go willingly into a far country, Egypt. He was sold into slavery. In that distant land he lost nothing but gained, as it were, everything, when he became 'prime minister' to the pharaoh (Gen. 37:1–36, 39–50). The stories of Jacob and Joseph are stories of winners and losers. The younger brothers win, the older brothers lose.

Jesus' story of the prodigal son offered a parody of such 'successful' younger brothers. In this story, the elder brother is not beaten or excluded. Far from losing, he is invited to take part in the family feast. Along with his brother he needs to be delivered from evil and enjoy a new family life. It is never said that the father loves the younger son more than the elder son. He loves both and cares for both in their different needs. All of this reflects Jesus' desire to establish a new brotherhood and sisterhood in the family of 'Abba': 'Whoever does the will of God is my brother and sister and mother' (Mark 3:35 parr.). From what Jesus has experienced of his loving Father, there are no losers, but only winners.

Clearly we should let ourselves be astonished by the story of the prodigal son, rather than kill it with close analysis. I feel impertinent when commenting on the amazing love of our compassionate God which comes through so powerfully.

Hearing and being drawn into this story is infinitely prefer-able to indulging in any comments. Yet we may be helped to appreciate the parable a little more by remembering how the divine love is merciful, welcoming, life-giving and the trigger of lasting joy. A little analysis shows how these characteristics of God's love shine through the longest and most beautiful story Jesus ever told, and they provide a rich help towards understanding what he meant by 'Abba', the word that opens the Lord's Prayer. 'Abba' is merciful, welcoming, life-giving and the source of lasting joy.

Even if (despite Gal. 4:6 and Rom. 8:15) he never clearly mentioned the Our Father, St Paul strikingly chose (or endorsed) love as the defining characteristic of the Father in a benediction with which he closed one of his letters: 'The grace of the Lord Jesus Christ, the love of God [the Father], and the communion of the Holy Spirit be with all of you' (2 Cor. 13:13). The order of this benediction is instructive. The grace or gift of Christ leads one to the love of 'Abba', the Father. That love, when realised through the power of the Holy Spirit, creates communion or fellowship with God and with one another.

Through various sections of Jesus' teaching we can fill out further what he knew God to be like. He taught that our heavenly Father actively cares for the whole of creation and, in particular, for all human beings, both innocent and wicked (Matt. 5:43–46): 'the Father in heaven makes his sun rise on the evil and on the good alike, and sends rain on the righteous and the unrighteous.' God is kind and merciful to all, even to 'the ungrateful and the wicked' (Luke 6:35). The providential concern of God extends to everyone and everything, includ-ing 'the lilies of the field' and 'the birds of the air' (Matt. 6:25–34; parallel in Luke 12:22–31). Jesus moved from the divine care for tiny sparrows to assure his audience of their precious value to God: 'Are not five sparrows sold for two pennies? Yet not one of them is forgotten in God's sight. But even the hairs of your head are all counted. Do not be afraid; you are of more value than many sparrows' (Luke 12:6–7; parallel in Matt. 10:29–31). Jesus compared 'Abba' to an ideal human father who provides bread, fish and the other things his children need and who always tries to give them the very best (Matt. 7:7–11; parallel in Luke 11:9–13). Seemingly Jesus called his own disciples 'infants' or 'little ones'. He comforted them with the thought that, like a good parent with little children, God never lets them out of sight (Matt. 11:25; 18:10, 14) and will protect them from harm.

Matthew, as we saw in the last chapter, liked to characterise 'Father' as 'heavenly' and apparently added the description here and there. All the same, Jesus at least sometimes spoke of 'your heavenly Father', as when he exhorted his disciples: 'Be perfect, therefore, as your heavenly Father is perfect' (Matt. 5:48). Describing 'Abba' as 'heavenly' also served to point to God being utterly good to all, with a loving goodness that 'binds everything together in perfect harmony' (Col. 3:14). Being perfect means being unlimited in goodness, and the Revised English Bible translation of Matthew 5:48 catches the force of Jesus' exhortation: 'There must be no limit to your goodness, as your heavenly Father's goodness knows no bounds.' This was to set the standard incredibly high. Yet Jesus promised that those who aimed to imitate the divine goodness would be helped by the Holy Spirit (Matt. 10:20; Luke 11:13).

The witness Jesus offered to 'Abba' throws light on the key word with which the Lord's Prayer begins. We have sampled some of that witness. Its climax comes in the parable of the prodigal son, with its astonishing picture of the father who forgets his dignity and runs to hug the son who has finally come home. But we would neglect an essential part of Jesus' witness to 'Abba', if we failed to include the way in which the behaviour and words of Jesus himself illuminate what 'Abba' was and is like. As we saw in the last chapter, the revelation of the Father went hand in hand with the revelation of the Son. John's gospel presents Jesus as saying: 'If you know me, you will know my Father also', and 'whoever has seen me has seen the Father' (John 14:7, 9). Even if historically Jesus may never have said these exact words, they have a clear basis in his ministry and summarise the thrust and significance of much that he said and did. He was the perfect 'image' of 'Abba' (Col. 1:15); on the visible scene he revealed the invisible 'Abba'. In the person and human life of Jesus, human beings met and meet the Father.

After all, the parable of the prodigal son, which speaks so loudly about the loving concern of God for the lost and sinful, was intended to defend the practice of Jesus himself against those who complained about him: 'This fellow welcomes sinners and eats with them' (Luke 15:2). Luke has gathered together in chapter 15 three stories that Jesus had told about loss, followed by a finding and great joy: the parables of the lost sheep, the lost coin and the lost son. Jesus told these stories (perhaps on separate occasions), and there is abundant evidence that 'righteous' people were scandalised by his regular table fellowship with public sinners, whom they expected him to avoid. The 'bad company' Jesus kept and his loving forgiveness towards sinners of all kinds drew criticism against Jesus. Yet that behaviour also mirrored the merciful concern of 'Abba' towards those who were spiritually and morally lost. But much more could be said to back up the Johannine conclusion: knowing and seeing Jesus entailed knowing and seeing the Father. Let me select three examples where the words and deeds of Jesus throw light on the 'Abba' whom he loved and revealed: Jesus' attitude towards children; his concern for the sick and the hungry; and his self-image as a mother hen.

First, in the rural society of ancient Galilee children were sent off as soon as possible to take care of sheep or to do other chores, so that they could become producers and no longer remain mere consumers. Since they did not know the Torah, they came low on the religious and social scale. But Jesus showed himself their special friend; they were drawn to the beauty and joy of his company. When his disciples wanted to keep them away, Jesus became indignant, took some children into his arms, blessed them, and declared that the kingdom of God belonged to them. Children heard him hold them up as models for adults, who were also called to open themselves to the message of the kingdom: 'Whoever does not receive the kingdom of God as a little child will never enter it' (Mark 10:13–16; parallels in Matt. 19:13–15 and Luke 18:15–17). To illustrate the new attitude to God he encouraged, Jesus singled out children. He expected everyone to show a trusting, childlike attitude towards their heavenly Father. For Jesus, the seeming incapacity of children turned out to be their greatest asset. The fact that they had nothing to give or show in order to enter the kingdom of heaven made them receptive to all that God offered them. They could accept and appreciate the unique gift which they had not worked to deserve. When Jesus cherished and praised children, he let us glimpse something of his Father, who also loves and embraces everyone and, in a particular way, little children.

Second, the concern of Jesus for the sick, the dead and the hungry also lets us see what 'Abba' is like. He sometimes worked miracles by a simple word of command (e.g. Mark 2:11–12; 3:5). But on other occasions he touched people before healing them. A leper, for instance, arrived and on his knees begged for help, saying to Jesus, 'If you choose, you can make me clean.' Jesus, we are told, was 'moved with pity, stretched out his hand, touched him, and said to him: "I do choose. Be made clean." Immediately the leprosy left him, and he was made clean' (Mark 1:40–42). The leper begged to be healed, but never asked Jesus to touch him. Yet Jesus would not perform the miracle without first reaching out and putting his hand on the ravaged face of the leper. In another story Mark reports how Jesus brought back to life the dead daughter of Jairus, a leader of a synagogue. Jesus took the dead girl 'by the hand', and only then said to her 'little girl, get up' (Mark 5:21–43). Such gestures from Jesus reveal much about the God who

27

reaches out to touch each one of us in our needs. We may cry out for help like the leper; or like the dead girl we may be unable to do even that. But the 'Abba' whom Jesus lovingly proclaimed is always ready to take the initiative in reaching out to touch and heal our lives. The words of John's gospel come into play here: 'Whoever has seen me has seen the Father' (14:9). To see these compassionate gestures of Jesus towards the sick and the dead is also to see the Father at work, and to know more vividly the 'Abba' of the Lord's Prayer.

And then feeding the hungry. Mark tells of Jesus and his core group of twelve going off by themselves to a deserted place, but finding on their arrival a huge crowd. Thousands of people wanted to see and hear Jesus. Yet they seemed lost and aimless – 'like sheep without a shepherd'. Jesus 'was moved with pity for them', taught them 'many things', and then fed them miraculously (Mark 6:30–44). The Revised English Bible renders the reaction of Jesus superbly: 'his heart went out to them.' It was the compassionate reaction of a mother, or at least the response of any loving parent. Once again the reaction of Jesus mirrored the way in which the heart of our motherly-fatherly divine 'Abba' goes out to the lost and the hungry.

Third, in a striking image Jesus compared his saving mission to the action of a mother hen gathering and protecting her chickens under her wings (Luke 13:34; parallel in Matt. 23:37). The OT background to this image is fascinating. One passage evokes a mother eagle with her young: God has carried the people, like an eagle who hovers over her young, to spread her wings, take them up, and bear them aloft on her pinions' (Deut. 32:11). Ruth 4:12 speaks of the protecting divine 'wings' without specifying what bird it has in mind. Likewise Isaiah pictures God protecting and delivering Jerusalem 'like birds hovering overhead' (Isa. 31:5). The passage is not specific, but clearly the prophet does not have in mind earthbound hens. There are two astonishing features in Jesus' use of the imagery: first, he applied to himself an OT picture which seems so far to have been used only of God; second, he gave the image a very homely twist by representing himself not as a mighty eagle but as a barnyard hen. This motherly image of Jesus reflected the 'Abba' from whom he came and to whom his whole life was oriented. If Jesus showed himself to be motherly and protective towards those who needed him, so too did and does the Father. To see and know Jesus the Mother hen is to see and know Abba the Mother hen.

A MOTHERLY FATHER

The motherly sense of what Jesus is like (and hence what the Father is like) also comes through in the way NT writers present the death and resurrection of Jesus. During his farewell discourse in John, the disciples were assured by Jesus that their sorrow will be replaced by a unique joy. To express his promise, he cited the experience of childbirth:

> 'You will weep and lament, but the world will rejoice; you will be sorrowful, but your sorrow will turn into joy. When a woman is in travail she has sorrow, because her hour has come. But when she is delivered of the child, she no longer remembers the anguish, for joy that a child is born into the world. So you have sorrow now, but your hearts will rejoice, and no one will take your joy from you.' (John 16:20–22)

At the crucifixion itself, so John informs his readers, the mother of Jesus was standing with two other women, her sister (Mary, the wife of Clopas) and Mary Magdalene. She said nothing, but stood there silently to see the end. Jesus gave her into the care of the beloved disciple with the words, 'Woman, behold your son' (John 19:25–27). On Easter Sunday Mary Magdalene found the tomb empty, passed on the news of her startling discovery, and returned to weep at the hollowed-out place where the corpse of Jesus had been laid. Then near the place of death and burial Jesus appeared to her and asked: 'Woman, why are you weeping?' (John 20:15). When he identified himself by calling Mary Magdalene by name, ecstatic joy replaced this woman's pain.

A feminine sequence emerges clearly from John's text. From the image of a woman in childbirth, we move to the mother standing with two other women by the cross to see her Son die. And we come finally to the woman whose sorrow was turned into joy. Near the tomb, that 'vessel' which received the body of Jesus and like a womb held it for three days, she encountered Jesus newly and gloriously alive. At times commentators on the gospels have contented themselves with merely 'factual' questions. How strong is the evidence that Jesus' mother attended the crucifixion? Did Mary Magdalene (and possibly other women) discover the tomb to be open and empty on the third day? Such questions of fact risk ignoring deeper levels of symbolic meaning in the gospel texts which relate the events of Good Friday and Easter Sunday. It may prove hard to catch this meaning in a net of words, but we should not bypass the task of reflecting on the feminine face of Jesus' death, burial and resurrection – a face which also lets us glimpse some characteristics of the God whom Jesus preached and revealed.

However, before drawing three reflections from John's text, I need to insert three disclaimers. First, the evangelist could not have *fully* appreciated the import and weight of the symbolic language that characterises his gospel. But the explicit intention of any author does not rigidly guide and limit later interpretation. Our understanding and application of what is in his or her texts can go beyond (but should not go against) what the original author intended to convey in writing for a particular audience.[2] Second, symbols can suggest, express and typify a whole range of meanings. But merely rational explanation can never hope to capture this range of meanings, let alone state some precisely defined meaning which, to everyone's agreement, sums up the text. Hence, just as I do not claim to pinpoint some theme consciously worked out by the evangelist, so I would not pretend to exhaust the symbolic meaning to be found in the text of John's gospel. Third, I realise that 'feminine' and 'masculine' are characteristics of being human. Even if a woman in her capacity to bear children and in other ways expresses for us the 'feminine', we should neither identify feminine with female nor masculine with male.

After these disclaimers let me make three tentative reflections on the feminine imagery in John's passion and resurrection story. First of all, women and feminine imagery surround the dying and rising of Jesus. From the appeal to the experience of childbirth in his final discourse, we move to the mother and the other women silently present at the place and event of death. Then near the tomb-womb one of these women becomes the first person to meet Christ in his new and final state of risen existence. Women enclose the whole mystery; and this suggests something about our prayerful access to Good Friday and Easter Sunday. To know this mystery we need to know it in a feminine way. We might adapt a famous remark by St Augustine of Hippo and say: show me a woman and she will understand Christ's death and resurrection.[3]

My second reflection on what I call the feminine face of the crucifixion and resurrection in John focuses on Jesus himself. Long before this gospel was written, OT books used the figure of birth pangs when they announced that God would finally act to save his people (e.g. Isa. 26:17–18; 66:7–14). In the event, the highpoint of this saving action takes the form of a crucifixion in which Jesus himself suffers birth pangs as he brings the whole human race to new life. His own image of a woman in labour whose sorrow will give way to joy when her baby is 'born into the world' is dramatically exemplified by Jesus himself. He is the woman whose hour has come and who must endure the anguish of birth. Through suffering the pain of Calvary, he has given new life to the world. His mother, his aunt and Mary Magdalene assist at the agonising childbirth.

In a letter to the troublesome Galatians, Paul reaches for the figure of a mother at childbirth to describe his own apostolic experience: 'My little children, with whom I am again in labour until Christ be formed in you' (Gal. 4:19). The use of such an image here and in John 16:20–22 encourages us to view Christ's decisive act of salvation within the same feminine perspective.

Church writers such as St John Chrysostom (d. 407) have seen the piercing of Jesus' body on the cross and the outpouring of blood and water (John 7:37–39; 19:34) as a parenting and even a motherly image (*Catecheses* 3.19). Christ not only gives rise to the Church like Adam giving rise to Eve (Gen. 2:21–23) but also nurtures his offspring like a mother feeding children with her milk. Jesus' unconditional love made various fathers of the Church and later writers move easily to the great paradigm of unconditional love, maternal love. Augustine, for instance, incorporates in his image of the motherly Christ the legend of the pelican who sheds her blood on her dead offspring and so dies in bringing them back to life (*Enarrationes in Psalmos*, 101.1.7–8). Augustine drew here on Jesus' picture of himself as a mother hen and moved to the pelican in the light of the Vulgate translation of Psalm 102:6, where the psalmist who is tormented by pain pictures himself as being 'like a pelican in the desert'. Centuries later Thomas Aquinas employed the same image in writing of the 'loving pelican, Jesus the Lord (*Pie pellicane, Iesu Domine*)' in his hymn 'Adoro te devote'.

Third, if we think of Jesus' own mother as the 'woman in travail', the immediate result of Calvary is her dead Son. Some artistic representations of the 'deposition' (or taking down from the cross) portray the body of Jesus as very much reduced in size. He lies in his mother's arms almost like a stillborn child. These artists may have spotted something in John's text that commentators missed. The crucifixion 'delivers' a dead child, who must be inserted into the tomb before he is finally born to the new life of his risen existence. It is only by passing through the grave that the Son of Mary becomes the 'first-born from the dead' (Col. 1:18).

'Pietà (pity)' is the name given to pictures or sculptures of the Virgin Mary holding the dead body of Jesus on her lap or in her arms, whether his body is life-size or much reduced. Western art has also produced many examples of something very similar: the 'Throne of Grace (*Gnadenstuhl*)'. Turning up for centuries in a painted or carved form, it shows the Father holding the cross with the Son dead on it (or the Father simply holding the body of the Son) with the Holy Spirit as a dove hovering between them. One cross links the three figures; their unity is also expressed by their being turned toward each other. Frequently, as in the version by El Greco (d. 1614), the dead body of the Son already hints at the luminosity of the coming resurrection. Examples of the 'Pietà' and the 'Throne of Grace' often strikingly resemble each other, and rightly so. One might say that at the death of Jesus the Father shows himself to be a woman in travail. The crucifixion 'delivers' his dead Son, who must be placed in the tomb-womb before being born to the gloriously new life of the resurrection. The death of Jesus, and not merely the words and deeds of his ministry, reveals the motherly face of his 'Abba'.

THE WIDER NT WITNESS AND BEYOND

We find God identified as 'Father' 254 times in the NT (with 4 other possible cases). The experience and example of Jesus gave rise to this development. Over this point Raymond Brown agrees with John Meier and quotes him to that effect: 'One is justified in claiming that Jesus' striking use of *Abba* did express his intimate experience of God as his own father and that this usage did make a lasting impression on his disciples.'[4] As we saw above, the preaching and deeds of Jesus constantly filled out, either directly or indirectly, what he knew the Father to be like. The compassionate Father of whom Jesus spoke knows our needs before we ask, cares for all, and forgives all, even the wickedly unjust and sinful. Jesus' Father-image subverted any oppressive, patriarchal notions of God as primarily or even exclusively an authoritarian figure. Jesus also revealed the divine mystery as the Father to whom he himself stood in a unique relationship as the Son. Acting with filial consciousness, he manifested the Father.

Then Jesus' resurrection (with the outpouring of the Holy Spirit) made him the eldest Son of the Father's new family (Rom. 8:29), a family now empowered to say the Lord's Prayer, address God as 'Abba', and share intimately in Jesus' relationship to the Father in the Spirit. Matthew's gospel ends with the command to baptise 'in the name of the Father, and of the Son and of the Holy Spirit' (Matt. 28:19), the point of departure for the rites of initiation and creeds that will take their structure around the confession of faith in the Father, Son and the Holy Spirit. The voices of the NT and the Christian tradition harmonise in presenting Father, Son and Holy Spirit as the primary (not exclusive) way of speaking about the tripersonal God. In particular, the early centuries of Christianity show how faith in Jesus as Son of God coincided with faith in God as Father. Thus St Hilary of Poitiers (d. 367) called 'the very centre of a saving faith' the belief 'not merely in God, but in God as Father, and not merely in Christ, but in Christ as the Son of God' (*De Trinitate* 1.17).

When the Trinity is named, God the Father functions validly if we align ourselves with the meanings communicated in that metaphor by the biblical witnesses (above all, by Jesus himself) and refuse to literalise it. It is these meanings that convey true information. 'Father' names personally the God revealed in Israel's history and known as the 'Abba' of Jesus' life, death and resurrection (together with the outpouring of the Holy Spirit). The 'Father' of the Lord's Prayer fixes the reference when Christians speak of God and what they believe the Trinity to be like. The language and meaning of 'Abba' emerged from Jesus' specific, historical experience of God. Once we agree that language and experience, while distinguishable, belong inseparably together, we would misrepresent Jesus' experience if we insisted on replacing his central language for God. Fidelity to Jesus and what he gave us in the Lord's Prayer require believers to name the first person of the Trinity primarily as 'Father', while acknowledging Jesus himself as the Son of God (while giving him, of course, other such titles as 'Lord' and 'Messiah').

By not arguing for an *exclusive* use of male names, I recognise that we do use and should also use other names: such as the gender-neutral name of 'Creator' for the first person of the Trinity and such a female name as 'Wisdom' for the second person. Many possibilities open up: the NT often designates God the Father as 'God' (in the form of *ho Theos*) and provides well over a hundred distinctive names for Jesus.[5] The question at issue is not the use of other names but rather both the primary way of naming the Trinity in trinitarian formulations and the name 'Father' with which the Lord's Prayer opens and which refers to the first person of the Trinity.

When we call God 'Father', we are not making a literal statement: that is to say, one in which we refer to a male parent and so use the word in its primary, biological sense. Nor are we introducing a simile: that is to say, using the word 'father' in its customary sense and merely comparing God with some characteristic of a male parent. Here, as elsewhere, metaphor asserts an identity that simile lacks. Hence it can create a more vivid impact than a mere simile, because it entails tension in being, literally speaking, partly false. The metaphor of God as Father conveys truth at the metaphorical level but falsity at the literal level: God is not a biological parent who existed before his Son came into existence. Indisputably, taking this metaphor literally – that is, forgetting that it is an extended use of language – can only result in a distorted and oppressive version of the first person of the Trinity. Setting such misuse aside, we need to add something more on the positive side. This particular metaphor communicates a challenge as well as truth.

As was pointed out in the last chapter, 'God is King' established itself as a predominant metaphor in the OT, occurring much more often than metaphors about God as Husband and Father. In naming the King of Israel, the OT praises God for doing what earthly kings should do but frequently fail to do. God feeds the hungry, protects strangers, supports widows and orphans, and sees that justice is done for the oppressed (e.g. Ps. 146:5–10). Far from being taken from common kingly conduct at the time, this picture of divine kingship stands in judgement over the repeated failure of Israel's human kings to secure the rights of the weak and defenceless. Similarly, the picture that Chapter 1 painted of the (rare) OT metaphor of God as Father, so far from being drawn from fatherhood as commonly practised in the ancient Middle East, reproves and criticises the harsh way many fathers acted towards their children. The metaphor 'God is Father' evaluates and finds wanting the standard practices of fathers in patriarchal societies. No human fathers can match the standard of compassionate love and constant care set by God. Recalling the tender providence of the divine Father, one can easily concur with the injunction of Jesus: 'Call no one your father on earth, for you have one Father, the one in heaven' (Matt. 23:9).

Some later books of the NT may seem to tamper with the ideal portrait of divine fatherhood to be drawn from the OT, from Jesus' proclamation of 'Abba' (whose non-patriarchal behaviour is illustrated by the parable of the prodigal son), and from the letters of Paul.[6] A household code of conduct that lists domestic virtues and has much in common with popular Hellenistic philosophy turns up in various deutero-Pauline letters – letters attributed to Paul but probably not coming directly from him – and other later letters (Eph. 5:21—6:9; Col. 3:18—4:1; 1 Tim. 2:8–15; 6:1–2; Titus 2:1–15; 1 Pet. 2:18—3:7). Normally arranged according to three sets of

superiors (husbands, parents and masters) and of corresponding subordinates (wives, children and slaves), such a
household code exhorts the first set to be responsible and the
second set to be obedient. The code receives a Christian perspective and motivation. Authority should be exercised with
understanding and love. Thus two passages call on fathers to
protect and encourage their children: 'Fathers, do not provoke
your children to anger, but bring them up in the discipline
and instruction of the Lord' (Eph. 6:4; see Col. 3:21).[7]

We should keep our distance from some aspects of these
domestic rules for patriarchal society that accepted, for
instance, the institution of slavery, even while we recognise
the idealised colour given to them by faith in Christ. But – and
this is especially relevant to the present chapter – no passage
suggests that human fatherhood, even when virtuously
practised according to the domestic code of conduct, provides
the source and standard for naming God 'Father'. Indeed, one
possible translation of Ephesians 3:14 would suggest the very
opposite, when it speaks of adoring 'the Father, from whom
all fatherhood in heaven and earth takes its name'. Whatever
exegesis we adopt here, one thing is clear: no NT example of a
household code even implies the message, 'You Christian
fathers represent God and your example shapes our proper
image of the Father in heaven.'

Christians of the NT period and the following centuries
experienced God as Father (e.g. Rom. 8:15; Gal. 4:6) and did
not draw their sense of 'Abba' from the patriarchal system of
the Greco-Roman culture, let alone from pagan images of the
divine. St Justin Martyr (d. c. 165), for instance, found the
father image of Zeus revolting: 'A parricide and son of a
parricide, being overcome by the love of evil and shameful
pleasures, he came into Ganymede and those many women
he seduced' (*First Apology* 21). Far from being a Christianised
version of such an unscrupulous and exploitative tyrant, 'the
heavenly Father desires the repentance of sinners, rather than
their punishment' (*First Apology* 15).

SAVING THE LORD'S PRAYER

It is one thing to explain and endorse the 'father-talk' with which the Lord's Prayer begins. But the whole prayer faces two further objections. Is it truly, as many claim, a summary of Jesus' kingdom message – for instance, about the double command of love? Second, what of Christianity as a story-telling community of disciples, who remembered and handed on the message of what Jesus said, did and suffered? Where is his story and passion in the 'Our Father'?

First, Jesus inherited from the OT faith a double command of love: 'You shall love the Lord your God with all your heart' and 'you shall love your neighbour as yourself' (Mark 12:28–34 parr.; see Deut. 6:5; Lev. 19:18). Jesus did something novel when he combined the hitherto separate love commands to form the heart of his moral message. Admittedly the Lord's Prayer makes no explicit reference to love. But both the three 'you' petitions (directed towards God) and the four 'we' petitions (concerning our needs) make no final sense unless love underpins them. Since we love God, we pray trustingly to our 'Abba' or 'dear Father' that his will be done and his name held holy. It is only love, sometimes only truly heroic love, that will make it possible to forgive those who have sinned against us. It is love for our fellow human beings that allows us to begin the Lord's Prayer by saying '*Our* Father'.

Second, Chapter 1 above recalled how addressing God as 'Abba' characterised the prayer life of Jesus right through to the end and his agonising prayer in Gethsemane: 'Abba, Father, for you all things are possible. Remove this cup from me. Yet, not what I will, but what you will' (Mark 14:36). This present chapter has illustrated how witnessing to 'Abba' in his preaching and activity Jesus filled out his image of 'Abba'. In the coming chapters we will see the various ways in which the petitions of the Lord's Prayer encapsulate much from the mission and message of Jesus. We can easily connect those petitions with the message of the kingdom which Jesus preached and dramatised in his own person. Right from its opening word, the Lord's Prayer invites us to remember how Jesus revealed the Father to us – through his life, death and resurrection from the dead (together with the outpouring of the Holy Spirit).

Chapter 3

◆

'OUR FATHER'

T HE 'OUR' WITH WHICH the Lord's Prayer opens in English was and is intended to be read in an inclusive sense.
St Matthew or – more likely – the tradition on which he drew
added 'our' to the original beginning of the prayer. Most
scholars think that Jesus simply opened the prayer with
'Abba/Father dear' (or 'my own dear Father'). Yet the 'our'
brings out what Jesus intended and wanted: a totally inclusive
prayer. The fatherly-motherly love of God includes and
encloses everyone in the one family of God.

AN INCLUSIVE 'ABBA'

The addition of 'our' to the opening of the Lord's Prayer also
brings out the way in which Paul, the first (in the NT writings)
and perhaps the greatest interpreter of Jesus and of Christian
faith, understood matters. The Apostle never quotes the 'Our
Father' as such, but that matches other features of the Pauline
correspondence. There were many things about Jesus (e.g. the
parables, the miracles and the preaching of the kingdom) and
the life of the early Christians which Paul knew but which he
never explicitly mentioned. He obviously joined in the cele-
bration of the Eucharist (1 Cor. 11:23–28), but he never spe-
cified the identity of those who presided at the Eucharist.

Paul never referred to the Lord's Prayer as such. But it would be foolhardy to claim that he did not know and use this prayer. He twice quoted the opening word and did so in its (original) Aramaic form, 'Abba'. The Apostle understood 'Abba' in an *inclusive* sense, as 'our' Father. Writing to some Celtic Christians in Galatia, he said: 'When the fullness of time had come, God sent his Son, born of a woman, born under the law, in order to redeem those who were under the law, so that *we* [inclusive] might receive adoption as sons and daughters. As proof that *you* [plural] are sons and daughters, God has sent the Spirit of his Son into *our* [plural] hearts, crying "Abba! Father!"' (Gal. 4:4–6). The 'we' and 'our' are clearly inclusive and collective. Paul thought not merely of Jews who had been born with the obligation to keep the law of Moses but also of some troublesome Celts who had been baptised and become Christians. All were sons and daughters of God; all had received into their hearts the Holy Spirit who enabled them to pray 'Abba'.

Paul's appeal to the Father in his Letter to the Romans was also inclusive and collective: 'When we cry "Abba! Father!" it is the Spirit witnessing with *our* spirit that *we* are sons and daughters of God' (Rom. 8:15). Once again it was a matter of 'we' and 'our [collective] spirit'. Paul's inclusive meaning was obvious. In the last chapter of the same letter, Paul would list 26 of those sons and daughters of God, who through the power of the Holy Spirit could cry out together 'Abba'. Some were men and some women; some were Jewish relatives of Paul himself, some Gentiles. The inclusive nature of the list matched beautifully what the Apostle had said earlier in Romans about the inclusive way in which early Christians prayed to God their 'Father'.

Yet it is not enough to use the words 'our' and 'we'. We must take these words in a truly inclusive sense and mean them in a genuinely inclusive way. Human beings persistently tend to take 'our' and 'ours' in an exclusive sense. I think here of someone (Julius Caesar) who, a few decades before Jesus and Paul were born, was busy conquering the Gauls and founding the Roman Empire. During a homily preached in the chapel of Newman College (University of Melbourne) in July 2001, Peter Steele cited the military memoirs of Julius Caesar, who referred constantly to the 'Roman soldiers as "ours": and the implication very clearly was that these "ours" were marked off from the barbarous, distasteful and expendable "theirs", whom he slaughtered in as large numbers as possible. This is the exclusive use of the word "ours" or "our".' Steele then applied his point to many religious traditions in which the central divinity has, at least from time to time, been portrayed in such exclusive terms: 'The god of the tribe, or of our nation, is our god: you can't have him, and he wouldn't want you – that is the spirit in which much history has been conducted.' Such religious exclusivism becomes ironically tragic when 'enemies who are at one another's throats' appeal to the same 'god'. As Steele recalled:

> Thousands of Christians ... have over the centuries appealed to Father, Son and Holy Ghost, while doing dreadful things to one another. At such moments, the attempt to seize on God as a partisan Lord is pathological. The word 'our', in such contexts, is symptomatic of a mortal disease.

In the 'Our Father', the word 'Our' runs in exactly the opposite direction, in a radically *inclusive* direction. God will not identify himself as the deity of a particular group at the expense of their enemies and even at the expense of the rest of humanity. Abba, the Father of all men and women, is utterly inclusive. As Steele put matters:

> 'Our Father' means 'the Father of all, the Father of any and all who can see themselves linked with the others: and even the Father of any and all who can't see any such thing'. It means, 'the Father of the conquerors and of the conquered; of the indifferent and the needy; of the pitiless and the pitiable; of absolutely everybody'.

To pray 'Our Father' surrenders any right to be exclusive. This prayer challenges us to give up the deep inclination we all have to close our eyes to and to keep away from those who notably differ from us and who apparently cannot serve our interests. In that way the opening words of the Lord's Prayer imply an examination of conscience. Do I close my eyes to those who are notably different from me? How does the 'Our' of 'Our Father' call on me to relate to others?

In Chapter 1 above, we noted how the closing section of Isaiah (56—66) contains two of the very few OT passages in which God is addressed as 'Father' and, in fact, is identified and addressed as 'Our Father' (Isa. 63:16; 64:6–8). The two chapters (63 and 64) deal primarily with Israel. What comes a little later could encourage reading the 'our' of these two passages in an inclusive, rather than an exclusive, sense. Right at the end of the Book of Isaiah, we come across one of the great passages from the Bible about God's active love towards all people, a vision of God revealing the divine glory to all nations (Isa. 66:18–23). It begins with God announcing: 'I am coming to gather the nations of every language. They shall come to witness my glory.' We might understand and interpret this promise in terms of our modern world and think of God saying: 'I am coming to gather the nations of every language, those who speak Mandarin, those who speak Hindi, those who speak English, those who speak Spanish, those who speak Arabic, and so forth.' That passage from Isaiah lists the nations as Tarshish, Put, Lud, Moshech, Rosh, Tubal and Javan. That is an exotic roll-call of names for ancient places. We could modernise the list and substitute other names: Beijing, Bangkok, Cairo, Caracas, Nairobi, Paris, Tokyo, Washington, and so forth. God is very upbeat about the divine plan to show all the nations his glory, and to bring all peoples together. In the words of Isaiah, the nations will come to Jerusalem and make their offerings in the Temple. They will arrive on horses, mules and camels, or riding in chariots, or being carried on litters. For these strangers and outsiders, God's plans are very inclusive and open-minded. God even intends to take some of these Gentiles and make them 'priests and Levites' to serve in the Temple. Then this new people of God will all join in a chorus of praise to God and will endure for ever. As far as God is concerned, there are no outsiders, only insiders.

For some or even many Israelites this had to be subversive, even intolerable, talk. How could their God reveal himself to all those outsiders? How could God gather together those outsiders in Jerusalem and accept their offerings and sacrifices? How could God go so far as even to make some of them priests and Levites to serve in the Temple along with the Jewish priests and Levites? For many Jews of the sixth century BC, it was a shocking message that the prophet communicated from God. How could God be so inclusive and welcoming to all? What had happened to the exclusive privileges of the chosen people? Those privileges, above all God's special relationship with the chosen people, were not being suppressed or taken back. God never revokes or takes back the divine gifts. God was and is greater than any of his gifts, and is never limited by what he has done, even by what he has done for the chosen people. God's love was and is shockingly inclusive and generous. In the case of Christians, through Christ and the Holy Spirit God has shared with all the baptised all kinds of wonderful gifts and graces. But Christ and the Spirit look beyond the members of the Church to a wider reality, the universal kingdom of God, which is divine salvation offered to all. God has been extraordinarily good to each of the baptised and blessed them amazingly. Yet God also cares most lovingly for everyone in the world. As far as God is concerned, there are no outsiders, only insiders. We might put this point in terms of a hymn by Paul Benoit ('Where Charity and Love Prevail') and its last line, 'Our family embraces all whose Father is the same.'

INDIVIDUALISM CHALLENGED

Perhaps the most revolutionary social change in the twentieth-century world was the shift around the globe from village life to urban life. Millions of people moved from the country to the city. Our huge cities can leave people in great isolation, or else encourage them to relate to others in ways that fall far short of any inclusive brotherhood and sisterhood. Relationships can be limited and guided by the principle, 'I will look after your interests if you look after mine.' The disvalues of the autonomous, ambitious self can quietly reign supreme. The Lord's Prayer sets its face against any such selfish individualism. This prayer is not an 'I' prayer and is not to be rewritten 'My Father'. It is from the outset a 'we' prayer. We come before God together and not primarily as individuals.

Let me turn bold here and offer a little suggestion for revising a text from St Augustine. Many of us are familiar with his prayer, 'Lord, that I might know myself, that I might know thee.' In the light of the Lord's Prayer which Augustine cherished and wrote about, he might have prayed: 'Lord, that we might know ourselves, that we might know thee.' Centuries after the time of Augustine, René Descartes decided to found his philosophy of knowledge on the principle, 'I think, therefore I am (*cogito, ergo sum*)'. He might have been better advised to have started with the principle, 'we think, therefore we are (*cogitamus, ergo sumus*)'. If Descartes had taken a line from the Lord's Prayer (which he knew from childhood), he could have written: 'We pray together; therefore we exist together as sons and daughters of the same loving Father.'

Whatever changes we might like to make in famous texts from Augustine and Descartes, the two first words of the Lord's Prayer settle for ever our proper relationship not only with God but also with other human beings. Since God is our common Father, then all our fellow human beings are our brothers and sisters. Our 'vertical' relationship to our loving

'Abba' must be matched by our 'horizontal' relationship with all the human beings who populate the planet earth. Thus God's fatherhood implies and calls for our active solidarity with each of the other men and women around us. Hence the opening address of the 'Our Father' excludes any indifference to the needs and concerns of others, let alone any readiness to exploit them and discriminate against them. 'Our Father' introduces the first of the 'you' petitions, which as such are directed towards God and what God does or will do. Even so, when applauding the divine deeds, we are praying to be changed ourselves.

THE CALL OF JESUS

Following Jesus means joining the family of God, whose paternal/maternal love sets him apart from even the very best of human parents. Jesus was remembered as saying: 'Do not call any man on earth "Father", for you have one Father, and he is in heaven' (Matt. 23:9). In this new family we never live or pray alone, as if we were isolated selves, but always as members of a community that our compassionate God cherishes and will cherish for ever.

Luke's version of the Lord's Prayer begins simply: 'Father'. Probably the 'our' in Matthew's version, as has been mentioned, does not literally go back to Jesus. But it certainly brings out what he implied and intended. He wanted all of us to be his brothers and sisters: adopted sons and daughters of God and joint heirs with Christ (Paul); children of God through the only Son (John).

THE PROTECTION OF ABBA

The 'Our' of 'Our Father' points then to an all-inclusive solidarity. The words also convey a sense of the common protection which our loving God offers us. Here I value something which parents of small children sometimes say to them at night. Children can be afraid of the dark and of 'things that go bump in the night'. When they become anxious and begin to cry, parents will get up, take their tiny children in their arms and sometimes assure them: 'Don't worry, darling. Everything is going to be all right.' When that happens and this unqualified promise is made, parents become living symbols of our heavenly Father. They remind me of our all-loving and all-powerful 'Abba'. God takes us all in the divine arms and says: 'Don't worry, darling. Everything is going to be all right.' That experience of what young parents do has often given me a little glimpse of the loving God who protects all of us and watches over all of us. Let me add a favourite story to drive home this point.

Caryll Houselander (1901–54), a wise spiritual guide to many, recalled an incident from the days when London was being attacked in the Second World War. A man was building a sandbag wall to protect a building against bomb blasts. Somehow Houselander dropped between the bags a crucifix that she was wearing. The stranger insisted on recovering it for her, even though it meant taking the wall of bags apart. Then he stood there holding her crucifix and looking at it with puzzled wistfulness. 'I'm a Jew,' he said. 'My mother was a good Jewess; I never learnt anything about Christ; we didn't bother to. But I did learn to say my prayers day and night, and I wish that I had kept it up.' When Houselander asked, 'What did you say?', he told her: 'Well, the morning ones were long, but the night prayer was short; all of us little Jewish kids said it as we fell asleep. It went like this: "Father, into thy hands I commend my spirit."' He added: 'It's what mothers are said to have taught little Jewish boys ever since the world began. They tell them to say that prayer just before they fall asleep.'[1]

According to Luke's gospel (23:46), Jesus said these words from Psalm 31:5 just before he fell asleep in death. In life and in death he commended himself totally into the hands of the all-loving 'Abba', the utterly caring God. Through life and at the time of death, we too can say that prayer: 'Father, into your hands I commend my spirit.' God is our Father, an infinitely loving God to every one of us.

FATHER ON DIFFERENT GROUNDS

Houselander's story hints at the different reasons for God being 'Father' to human beings. First, all human beings can call God 'Father', because he is their Creator (Isa. 64:8; Mal. 2:10). Every human person can say that in God we 'live and move and have our being' (Acts 17:28). Second, Jews should call God 'Father' because of their election as the chosen people and salvation from Egypt in the whole Exodus event. Non-Jews do not have these grounds for giving God that name. Third, Christians call God their 'Abba' on the basis of their faith in Christ and baptism. They have received the gift of the Holy Spirit, the Spirit of adoption as God's sons and daughters (Rom. 8:14–17), and have been conformed to the risen Jesus as their elder brother (Rom. 8:28–30). This is the special way in which God is now their 'Father' and they can pray the Lord's Prayer.

Hence in the early Church, part of the initiation process for prospective converts included learning the Lord's Prayer. They were allowed to pray it with the community for the first time only in the eucharistic service following their baptism. The 'Our Father' was a sign of their identification as Christians. As baptised members of the Church, they now enjoyed the privilege of praying the Lord's Prayer, saying 'Our Father' in this new way and inviting others to join them in doing so through faith and baptism.

Chapter 4

'IN THE HEAVENS'

MILLIONS AND MILLIONS OF Christians pray together every Sunday in their church worship, 'Our Father who art in heaven'. This reverential address, found in Matthew's but not in Luke's version of the Lord's Prayer, works particularly well when said or sung together in unison. The phrase adds a certain reverence to the opening words, 'Our Father'.

JESUS' HEAVENLY FATHER

Even if 'in the heavens' derives from Matthew or from a tradition on which he drew, the sentiment goes back to Jesus himself. At least sometimes he spoke of God as 'heavenly'. He insisted that his followers match their words with deeds: 'Not everyone who says to me, "Lord, Lord", will enter the kingdom of heaven, but only the one who does the will of my Father in *heaven*' (Matt. 7:21). On another occasion Jesus cried out with joy: 'I thank you, Father, Lord of *heaven* and earth, because you have hidden these things from the wise and the intelligent and have revealed them to infants' (Luke 10:21). These and some further sayings arguably come from Jesus, and echo the heavenly scenario of many psalms that he had learnt to pray. God 'sits in the heavens' (Ps. 2:4), and is to be praised 'in his mighty heavens' (Ps. 150:1).

The author of that final psalm wants God to be reverenced and worshipped with a whole range of musical instruments: lutes, harps, tambourines and cymbals. Psalm 150 is full of reverence and worship. It may well have helped inspire a wonderful work of art in the city hall of Siena, Italy. On the choir stalls in the chapel of that city hall, a fifteeenth-century artist, Domenico Spinelli di Niccolò, has left twenty-two wooden inlays to illustrate the articles of the creed. They are magnificent pieces of mosaic woodwork. The last of them represents eternal life with God. It does so by portraying angels devoted to reverent worship and playing various musical instruments before God. Spinelli evidently imagined heaven as a reverent, sacred concert that will never end.

Our Father 'in the heavens' is the 'Holy One' or the 'Utterly Other', who will feature in the next petition of the Lord's Prayer. As the 'Heavenly One', God is not earthly and visible but distinct and beyond all created things. Yet even in the OT, this holy 'otherness' of God did not exclude a deep sense of the divine nearness. Our God is utterly other, and at the same time totally near to us. Early chapters of Deuteronomy (4—7) yield that double feeling about the Holy One. They evoke a sense of the awesome, heavenly otherness of God, who is, nevertheless, close to his people. On Mount Sinai the Lord speaks out of the fire, the cloud and the thick darkness (Deut. 5:22). No wonder then that Moses calls the Lord the 'great and awesome God' (Deut. 7:21). At the same time, however, Moses can put the question: 'What other nation has a god so near to it as the Lord our God is, whenever we call to him?' (Deut. 4:7). Moses assures the people: 'The Lord is present' (Deut. 6:15); 'the Lord has set his heart on you' (Deut. 7:7). Moses pulls together the two aspects of God: 'The Lord your God, who is present to you, is a great and awesome God' (Deut. 7:27).

We see the same double aspect of God expressed in the early chapters of Isaiah. Isaiah 6 reports the call of the prophet, who hears seraphs calling to each other: 'Holy, holy,

holy is the Lord of hosts; the whole earth is full of his glory' (Isa. 6:3). By repeatedly invoking 'the Holy One of Israel' (Isa. 1:4; 5:19, 24; 10:20; 17:7; 29:19; 30:11, 12, 15; 37:23) the prophet wants to emphasise how God is separate and 'beyond'. Even so, God is far from unapproachable. The prophet sings of the divine presence in the Temple: 'great in your midst is the Holy One of Israel' (Isa. 12:6). By choosing with gracious love the people of Israel, God remains always tenderly close to them. Such language from Isaiah can turn easily into prayer addressed to God: 'You are the Holy One; you are great in our midst.' It is no wonder then that the Book of Isaiah has sometimes been called the Fifth Gospel.

Jesus himself inculcated a reverent awe for God. When cleansing the Temple, he showed how outraged he was that the holy Temple of God was defiled by trading (Mark 11:15–17). Yet the God he preached was 'the heavenly Father', who cares deeply for all his creatures, even for tiny sparrows who were sold for less than a penny (Luke 12:6–7; parallel in Matt. 10:29–31). The distinct and awesome 'otherness' of God our Father does not stand in the way of his caring closeness. In the Acts of the Apostles, Luke pictures St Paul making the same point in a speech on the Areopagus. On the one hand, God is 'Lord of heaven and earth' who cannot be confined to 'shrines made by human hands'. Yet, on the other hand, it is in God that 'we live and move and have our being' (Acts 17:24, 28). This image recalls the first nine months of our human existence when we were all umbilically bonded to our mother. She provided us with a quiet and safe 'space' in which to live and grow. There is a receptive, nurturing and maternal feel to the divine presence evoked by Paul.

A few centuries later St Augustine of Hippo (d. 430) knew God to be supremely mysterious and 'beyond' our material world. Yet the heavenly Father, as Augustine appreciated, is 'closer' to us than we are to ourselves. Augustine said to God in his *Confessions*: 'But you were more inward than my inmost self (*tu autem eras interior intimo meo*)' (3.6.11).

51

From medieval times, Christian artists have been encouraged by the representation of God as 'the Ancient One' (Dan. 7:9) to portray the heavenly Father as a bearded old man seated on clouds or emerging above some clouds. Thus Titian's *The Holy Trinity* in the Prado (Madrid) depicts God the Father sitting on clouds and holding a sphere (representing the whole created world) and facing the Son who is also seated on clouds. Presiding over them at the centre is the Holy Spirit, symbolised as a luminous dove. Below, human beings are being drawn tumultuously upwards towards the Trinity. For Titian, God is ruling majestically 'in the heavens', yet human beings are being drawn dynamically towards him.

In his *Baptism of Christ*, now in Vicenza (Italy), Giovanni Bellini adds to the story as we have it from Mark, followed by Matthew and Luke. Three angels attend the baptism – a detail presumably added to emphasise the Trinity. The evangelists report only a mysterious, awesome voice from heaven which lovingly approves of 'my beloved Son'. Bellini gives the Father a face and depicts him as breasting some clouds and looking down on the scene of Christ's baptism. Whatever the artistic merits of such works by Titian, Bellini and others, the Father 'in the heavens' is awesome but has lost some of his mysteriousness. For a thousand years Christian art remained very reverent and did not dare to represent the Father with a human face and body. At most there would be a hand reaching down to facilitate the ascension of Jesus. God is powerfully and lovingly present, but still mysterious.

CHRISTIAN PILGRIMAGE

While the opening words of the Lord's Prayer, 'Our Father in the heavens', form an address to God, they also say something about God. The words 'in the heavens' also hint at the point and purpose of all human life: our movement home to God. The whole Jewish-Christian story has also expressed that movement through the theme of pilgrimages. Abraham and

Sarah left Ur of the Chaldees and became nomads for God. Some NT writings saw life as a journey of 'exiles' (1 Pet. 1:1) to a heavenly homeland (Phil. 3:20). The Letter to the Hebrews, in particular, developed this theme in chapter 11. Hebrews gives us a roll-call of heroes and heroines of faith, and comments on them: 'They confessed that they were strangers and foreigners on earth. People who speak in this way make it clear that they are seeking a homeland ... they desire a better country, that is, a heavenly one' (Heb. 11:13–16). Cultivating a sense of our human existence as a *pilgrimage* home to 'Our Father in the heavens' is a desirable way to live.

By AD 250 the popular cult of Peter and Paul (and of other martyrs) began to flourish in Rome and draw pilgrims to their tombs. Such pilgrimages continued and grew when the persecutions ceased and Constantine helped to make Christianity the official faith of the Empire. Along with Jerusalem and Santiago de Compostela (with its tomb of St James the Apostle), Rome continued to attract pilgrims, especially after the Jubilee years began in 1300. Dante, who came to Rome for that first Jubilee, used the pilgrimage theme to open the *Divine Comedy* ('In the middle of our life's road I found myself in a dark wood – the straight way ahead lost'). In Dante's *Comedy* the spiritual transformation of the pilgrim takes him through hell and purgatory to heaven. It is a midlife pilgrimage that Dante wrote about, a journey during one's middle years that has characterised the lives of many outstanding Christians.[1]

A few years after Dante, Geoffrey Chaucer (1340–1400) pictured in *The Canterbury Tales* a group of 29 pilgrims on their way to the shrine of St Thomas Becket (d. 1170) in Canterbury Cathedral. In the Middle Ages these shared journeys to the shrines of saints embodied a common faith and strengthened a common feeling for the purpose of life.[2] Stone crosses along the roads made the journey sacred, and at the journey's end the venerated sanctuary renewed the sense of communion with Christ, with his saints and with the 'Father in the heavens'. The ancient Celts named such shrines 'thin places'; time and again in those 'thin places' they experienced a close communion between God and themselves.

Such pilgrimages reinforced the consciousness of life as a spiritual journey, a preparation for death and eternal life. *Everyman*, an English morality play of the late fifteenth century, reflected that sense. The hero encounters the person of Death, who summons him to God and judgement. The changing seasons of Advent, Christmas, the Epiphany, Lent, Holy Week, Easter and Pentecost also played their part in sustaining the feeling of human life moving through sacred time to a final meeting with God, 'our Father in the heavens'.

Part 2

◆

THE 'YOU' PETITIONS

Chapter 5

◆

'MAY YOUR NAME BE MADE HOLY'

T HIS, THE FIRST OF the 'you' petitions, asks that the holiness of God's name be vindicated, and is arguably the most Jewish of all the petitions in the Lord's Prayer. I say that for four reasons. They are four biblical and spiritual reasons.

A JEWISH PETITION

First, the grammatical construction (passive voice) used in 'be made holy' recurs over and over again in the OT to indicate implicitly and reverently a divine action but without explicitly naming God. Thus the full sense of the petition is: 'May your name be made holy *by you.*'

In the NT we come across a similar reverent reference to God's action in Mark's account of what Mary Magdalene and her two companions found when they reached the tomb of Jesus on the first Easter Sunday: 'They saw that the stone had been rolled away' (Mark 16:3). The reader is expected to understand that the stone had been rolled away 'by God'. When St Paul reaches the punchline of a very early formula of Christian proclamation, he declares that Christ 'has been raised on the third day according to the scriptures' (1 Cor. 15:4). Attentive readers know that Christ has been raised 'by God'. Here and in numerous other places Jesus and the authors of the NT use this reverent, implicit way of indicating some divine action, and in doing so they remain faithful to their Jewish, OT roots.

That way of reverently referring to the divine agency is also a lovely hint of God's action in our lives. God is very discreet. We are being made holy by God, and we might hardly notice what God is doing. We can face some huge problem, and there seems to be no exit. But then we find that the stone has been rolled away or is being rolled away. We may feel ourselves to be dead and lacking in spiritual vitality, and suddenly we realise that we have been revived by God. This Jewish way of implicitly and reverently indicating the divine action found in the first petition of the Lord's Prayer enjoys its real counterpart in our personal story and in God's discreet way of acting to change that story.

Second, 'hallowed be your name' evokes the utter reverence the OT constantly displays towards the sacred Tetragrammaton, the Hebrew name for God written in four letters (YHWH) and apparently meaning 'he causes to be'. According to the Book of Exodus, the name was revealed to Moses when he saw a marvellous flame of fire out of a burning bush and unexpectedly found himself in a holy place (Exod. 3:1–16). As is well known, when Jews came to the YHWH in the biblical texts, they did not pronounce it but substituted 'Lord (*Adonai*)' or '*Kyrios*' (in the Greek translation). Christians do well to share something of the Jewish sense of utter reverence towards God and the name of God, and could pray: 'You are our Lord, our Holy One, our *Adonai*'.

The Psalms, in particular, prompt a third reflection on 'may your name be made holy'. Praise and salvation were frequently linked to the 'name' of the Lord – a further dimension in the Jewish background to Jesus' choice of 'your name' for the first petition of the Lord's Prayer. When delivered from some fears and troubles, the psalmist invited his congregation: 'O magnify the Lord with me, and let us exalt his *name* together' (Ps. 34:3). Sung at the Passover festival before the meal, Psalm 113 expressed the choral response this way: 'Blessed be the *name* of the Lord from this time on and forevermore. From the rising of the sun to its setting, the *name* of the Lord is to be praised' (Ps. 113:2–3). Praising the name of God was a language of prayer that was familiar to Jesus. So too was the theme of salvation for those who called upon the name of the Lord (Joel 2:32). Jesus knew the psalm which spoke of prayer in a serious illness: 'I called on the name of the Lord: "O Lord, I pray, save my life".' His prayer for recovery heard, the psalmist turned to thank God: 'I will offer to you a thanksgiving sacrifice and call on the name of the Lord' (Ps. 116:4, 17). Another psalm prayed for deliverance from national enemies: 'Help us, O God of our salvation, for the glory of your *name*; deliver us, and forgive our sins, for your *name's* sake' (Ps. 79:9).

In a real way, by proposing for prayer 'hallowed be your name' or 'may your name be made holy', Jesus was pulling together a constant theme in the psalms. He knew the psalms well and used them in prayer. We can fill out the thrust of 'hallowed be your name' by taking up psalms that *praise the name* of the Lord and seek *salvation* in the name of the Lord – like Psalm 116: 'I will raise the cup of salvation and call on the name of the Lord' (v. 13).

Finally, the holiness of God is a central divine attribute for OT faith: God is awesome and awesomely holy. In the Temple, under pain of death, no one could enter the Holy of Holies except the High Priest and then only once a year on the great Day of Expiation (Yom Kippur). In the Book of Leviticus we find the Code of Holiness (17—26), with its repeated injunction: 'You shall be holy, because I, the Lord, am holy.' Holiness emerges as a central divine attribute in the OT. This is a fourth reason for recognising the deep Jewish piety in the first of the 'you' petitions of the Lord's Prayer, 'May your name be made holy.'

JESUS AND THE HOLINESS OF GOD

Jesus might have left a slightly different prayer as the first of the 'you' petitions: 'May your name be praised.' After all, the psalms, with which he prayed repeatedly, sing praise to God – right through to Psalm 150 which wants trumpets, lutes, harps, tambourines and other musical instruments to contribute to a chorus of praise to God: 'Praise him with clanging cymbals, praise him with loud, clashing cymbals. Let everything that breathes praise the Lord!' (Ps. 150:5–6). Jesus hoped that the good deeds of his followers would lead others to praise God: 'Let your light shine before others, so that they may see your good works and give glory to your Father in heaven' (Matt. 5:16). The healing miracles worked by Jesus led those present to 'praise' and glorify God (e.g. Mark 2:12 parr.; Luke 17:15). If Jesus had changed the first 'you' petition to 'May your name be praised', that would have shifted the Lord's Prayer closer to some traditional strands of Christian piety. St Ignatius Loyola (d. 1556), for instance, in the 'First Principle and Foundation' of his Spiritual Exercises expressed the purpose of creation as follows: 'Human beings were created to *praise*, reverence, and serve God our Lord' (no. 23).

The praise of God is something to be expected from human beings. 'Making holy', however, belongs primarily to God and the divine action; it goes even deeper than human praise. Here the first 'you' petition of the Lord's Prayer lines up with and summarises the words of God reported by Ezekiel: 'I will prove my greatness and *holiness*, and make myself known in the sight of many nations; thus they shall know that I am the Lord' (Ezek. 38:23). For the sake of his 'holy name', God promises to cleanse and restore his people (Ezek. 36:22–32). It is only God who can 'make' or prove himself holy or prove his name holy by revealing himself as he is: that is to say, by manifesting his divine power, glory and holiness.[1] This self-manifestation of God, so Ezekiel expected, would gather the scattered tribes of Israel and establish the rule of God fully and for ever. It is to be a complete, definitive revelation of the divine holiness, directed to all nations. It is God who would 'make holy his name' and thus make known and glorify the divine self. It is God alone who can rightly and fully manifest himself in all his power and glory.

Thus in the first 'you' petition of the Lord's Prayer, Jesus pulls together the message of Ezekiel with unique precision: 'May your name be made holy.' Yet there are areas in which Jesus showed no desire to follow Ezekiel: for instance, in the prophet's language about being 'defiled like a woman in her menstrual period' (Ezek. 36:17) and other imagery that demeans women. The personality of Ezekiel comes across as distinctive, if not bizarre, and even repellent (see e.g. chapters 16 and 23). The capture and destruction of Jerusalem in 587 BC led to the disorienting experience of the exile in Babylon. As a prophet to the exiles, Ezekiel in his double role as priest and prophet assured the people of the abiding presence among them of their just and holy God, who will restore them to their homeland and Temple. For all his strangeness, Ezekiel treasured the holiness of God and deserved to be a major source for the first 'you' petition in the Lord's Prayer.

THE CHALLENGE OF HOLINESS

As much as, or even more than, any other petitions in the 'Our Father', 'May your name be made holy' focuses on God and the divine activity. Nevertheless, this petition also carries daunting challenges for human beings. It makes drastic demands on those who say these words in prayer. God's name is 'hallowed' by those in whose lives, through divine grace, the power of sin has been overcome. We are praying for a change in ourselves, not in God. Centuries earlier the Book of Leviticus offered its central injunction: 'You shall be holy, for I the Lord your God am holy' (Lev. 19:2).

Rudolf Otto left an account of the divine holiness that has long ago achieved classic status. In *Das Heilige* (first published

1917; ET *The Idea of the Holy*, 1958) he wrote of 'the frightening and fascinating mystery (*mysterium tremendum et fascinans*)'. God's utter holiness should trigger us into awed silence and profound reverence. Yet this 'fear' of God should be tempered by the deep intimacy that flows from being sons and daughters of our common Father.

In his letters to various communities, St Paul repeatedly recalled the holy gifts which they had received and the holy life to which they were called. Writing to the church of Philippi, he began by addressing 'all the holy ones in Christ Jesus' (1:1). The case of the Christians in Corinth is intriguing and instructive. Despite all the things that Paul wanted to correct in their practice and version of the new faith, he addressed them, nevertheless, as 'the church of God in Corinth, made holy by [God] in Christ Jesus [and] called holy ones' (1 Cor. 1:2). In his Second Letter to the Corinthians, the Apostle faced a somewhat different set of problems. Yet he could still address them as 'the church of God in Corinth and all the holy ones in the whole of Achaia' (the southern Roman province of Greece) (2 Cor. 1:1). No matter what the sins and problems he had to confront, Paul knew that those in the churches he had founded had been drawn irrevocably into communion with the holy God. Living out of that gift was the deepest challenge of their lives.

Paul is by no means the only NT author who writes this way. The Letter to the Hebrews, for instance, makes a spirited call to live lives of faith, love and *holiness*. Our whole destiny is at stake. As Hebrews puts it, 'pursue peace with everyone, and the holiness without which no one will see God' (Heb. 12:14). 'With a true heart' we can follow Jesus, confidently approach God and enter the very sanctuary of God. This means having 'the confidence' to do what the OT forbade under pain of death – namely, enter the Holy of Holies and see God (Heb. 10:19–22). There is a clear hint here of the beatitude: those who are holy and 'pure of heart' will 'see God' (Matt. 5:8).

'May your name be made holy', the first petition of the Lord's Prayer, enjoys many echoes in the OT and NT. It also calls to mind various liturgical prayers, such as the ancient lines sung on Good Friday during the veneration of the cross: 'Holy is God, holy and strong. Holy, immortal One, have mercy on us.' The petition evokes some familiar hymns, like the one based on the Liturgy of St James, 'Let all mortal flesh keep silence/ and with fear and trembling stand,/ ponder nothing earthly minded:/ for with blessing in his hand,/ Christ our God on earth descendeth,/ our full homage to demand.'

Jesus asked his followers to pray, 'May your name be made holy.' He himself was that holiness in person. Nothing suggests this better than the confession made by Peter in John's gospel: 'we have come to believe and know that you are the Holy One of God' (John 6:69).

Chapter 6

♦

'MAY YOUR KINGDOM COME'

I N THE SECOND 'YOU' petition we pray for the coming of the final kingdom of God – something we cannot achieve but which only God can make happen. The 'kingdom of God' is a slightly more abstract way of speaking of God ruling as king. So we pray equivalently: 'Come, O Father, to rule as king.' We reach here the very heart of Jesus' preaching, activity and suffering: the kingdom or rule of God. There is a straight line from what is central in the ministry of Jesus to the second petition in the prayer he shared with his disciples.

ALREADY AND NOT YET

Jesus proclaimed a divine kingdom that had already become effectively present through his deeds and words. When challenged about the source of the power with which he delivered people from demons, he replied: 'if it is by the finger of God that I cast out demons, then the kingdom of God has come upon you' (Luke 11:20 par.). Through his own person, Jesus himself was the presence of the divine kingdom. He called blessed those who were guided by faith to recognise in him (and in his words and deeds) the fulfilment of the divine purpose for the chosen people and for the world: 'Blessed are the eyes which see what you see! For I tell you that many prophets and kings desired to see what you see, but did not see it, and to hear what you hear, but did not hear it' (Luke 10:23 par.).

The kingdom of God, already initiated by the coming of Jesus, will be definitively realised and will be recognised everywhere and by everyone. Hence we are to ask in the Lord's Prayer that, once and for all at the end of time, God will reveal himself as the Father who wishes to save all people. The focus here is on God coming in the final future to rule as king. In effect, we pray: 'Father, reveal yourself in all your power and glory, by coming to rule as king.' In that way the doxology that was added to Matthew's text of the Lord's Prayer ('for yours is the kingdom, the power and the glory forever and ever. Amen') brings out the sense of the second 'we' petition. The power and glory of God characterise the divine kingdom, for the coming of which we pray.

The Lord's Prayer encourages us here to 'locate' God in the future. In the Book of Revelation we read: '"I am the Alpha and the Omega," says the Lord God, who is and who was and who *is to come*' (Rev. 1:8). This verse does not describe God as we might expect as the One who is and who was and who will be – that is to say, as equally related to the past, the present and the future. No, the verse presents 'the Lord God, who is and who was and who is to come'. The Book of Revelation, like the second 'you' petition in the 'Our Father', highlights the coming God, the God of the future. We could well turn the words of Revelation into a prayer: 'You are the Alpha and the Omega, the Lord God, who is and who was and who is to come.'

'Locating' God in the future means respecting the divine initiative which goes beyond anything we can plan and manipulate. Taught by experience, we know that what will in fact happen consistently goes beyond our predictions. The future introduces the element of the unmanageable and the unpredictable. There is no key to the present situation that will infallibly reveal how the future must evolve. In acknowledging the 'futurity' of our God and his coming kingdom, we are acknowledging the divine freedom and creativity that elude and transcend all human control and knowledge.

Scholars have written seemingly endless pages about the expectations the first Christians entertained about the end of history. Sometimes the gospel writers and Paul seem to anticipate the coming of the final kingdom within set time limits. Mark recalls Jesus saying to his disciples and some others 'There are some standing here who will not taste death until they see that the kingdom of God has come with power' (Mark 9:1). A little later, a discourse of Jesus in Mark 13 on the end of the age and its portentous signs appears to offer a similar, fairly precise calendar: 'this generation will not pass away until all these things have taken place' (Mark 13:20). Yet suddenly in this same chapter this calendar is balanced or even cancelled out: 'About that day or hour no one knows, neither the angels in heaven, nor the Son, but only the Father' (Mark 13:32). Hence Mark concludes this chapter with a warning about the unknowable time that will see the coming of God's final kingdom. We need to keep alert and 'watch' at every moment (Mark 13:33–37).

In this connection it is worth recalling Rudolf Otto's classic account of the Holy ('the frightening and fascinating mystery') that we saw in the last chapter and giving it a fresh application. God is the unpredictable mystery of the future that is both terrifying and enthralling. The future engages us and attracts us with the seemingly unlimited possibilities it holds out. It is at the same time fearful because it is so far unknown and in many ways uncontrollable. God is this numinous power of the future, the One who will not be fully our God and Father until the final kingdom comes.

From 1974 to 2006, I lived at the Gregorian University in Rome. For over thirty years Italians and their country have blessed me in so many ways and not least through their enchanting language. One of its advantages consists in having (like German and some other languages) two words for the future: *futuro* and *avvenire*. Where *futuro* and, for that matter, our English word 'future' can too readily suggest something growing out of the present, *avvenire* like 'Advent' points to the arrival or coming to us of something or, better, of Someone who is approaching us. *Avvenire* and 'Advent' create the sense of expectancy which sustains the petition 'May your kingdom come'. Every year, every day, is bringing God near to us. God is coming to enlighten and redeem us.

JESUS AND THE KINGDOM

Jesus, as we saw above, identified himself with the powerful reality of the kingdom already present on the human scene. He also associated himself with the future kingdom of God, doing so particularly through his self-designation as 'Son of Man'. Thus he warned his disciples and others: 'Those who are ashamed of me and of my words in this adulterous and sinful generation, of them the Son of Man will also be ashamed when he *comes* in the glory of the Father with the holy angels' (Mark 8:38). At the Last Supper, he looked forward to the new relationship between God and human beings which would come through his death and resurrection: 'I will never drink of the fruit of the vine until that day when I drink it new in the Kingdom of God' (Mark 14:25 par.). According to Mark, when Jesus appeared before Caiaphas a few hours later, he replied to the question 'Are you the Messiah, the Son of the Blessed One?', by combining Daniel 7:13 and Psalm 110:1 and declaring: 'I am; and you will see the Son of Man seated at the right hand of the Power [God], and *coming* with the clouds of heaven' (Mark 14:61–62).

In view of such memories about Jesus, we can understand how early Christians not only preserved the petition addressed to the Father 'May your kingdom come' but also transposed it into the personal key of Jesus. Paul ended one letter with a prayer in Aramaic that comes out of Palestinian

Christianity: 'Our Lord, Come! (*Marana tha*)' (1 Cor. 16:22). In Greek the same prayer appears at the close of the Book of Revelation: 'Come, Lord Jesus' (Rev. 22:20). A few chapters earlier that same book describes the victory of Christ and his heavenly army over the forces of evil (Rev. 19:11–21). He is named 'the King of kings and Lord of lords' (Rev. 19:16; see 17:14).

All this language preserved and developed by early Christianity helps to justify the way Ignatius Loyola took up 'the Kingdom of Christ' as a key contemplation in his Spiritual Exercises. He pictures 'Christ our Lord, the Eternal King' gathering together the whole world and addressing each and everyone as follows: 'It is my will to conquer the whole world and all my enemies, and thus to enter into the glory of my Father. Therefore, whoever wishes to join me in this enterprise must be willing to labour with me, that by following me in suffering, he may follow me in glory' (no. 95). This summons to 'the service of the eternal King and Lord of all' matches the call to accept the message of God's kingdom made by Jesus in his earthly ministry. To accept the coming rule of God was to become his follower and join him in the service of the kingdom. In a number of his parables Jesus opens up a vision of how human beings should respond to God's offer, accept the divine rule, and pray with total sincerity 'may your kingdom come'. It means praying: 'May your kingdom come; I want to be part of it; and that means I want to follow you.'

ACCEPTING THE KINGDOM

Let us take one parable about accepting the kingdom, the treasure in a field: 'The kingdom of heaven is like treasure hidden in a field, which someone found and hid; then in his joy he goes and sells all that he has and buys that field' (Matt. 13:44). First, the parable speaks of the immeasurable value of something which comes as pure gift. It is not something the finder (perhaps a poor labourer) had ever worked for and expected. The divine kingdom enjoys an incalculable worth like some magnificent treasure buried years before out in a field, perhaps when an invading army threatened to overrun the land and plunder everything within sight. The treasure God offers in the kingdom is colossal, and yet utterly free. No one needs to earn it; no one can earn it.

Second, suddenly blundering on the treasure changes the whole world for the fortunate finder. This totally unexpected stroke of good fortune turns his life around and fills him with ecstatic joy. For the lucky man all things have been made new.

Third, the finder must sacrifice everything if he is going to gain the treasure. He needs to 'sell all that he has', if he wants to buy the field which hides the immensely valuable prize he has stumbled on. The treasure is there for the having, and the field is apparently up for sale.[1] But first the lucky finder must convert into cash the small amount of property he currently owns. He needs to sell everything, if he is going to secure everything or rather more than everything.

Fourth, it goes without saying that the chance of gaining such a treasure turns up very rarely or only once in a lifetime, if even that. Finding a hidden hoard of gold gives us a chance that may never come again. Those who find such caches must instantly take advantage of their opportunity. They have to trust their quick judgement that the treasure is worth gaining at any cost and by any means. Immediately risking all and giving up all will make it possible to enjoy something that is truly a unique godsend.

As much as any of his other parables, Jesus shows here that the kingdom is something which comes to us from God and yet is also an amazing adventure that we must undertake. The kingdom is an incredible godsend, something that is completely and entirely God's work. And, at the same time, we should also realise that it is our affair, the perfectly good thing that turns up on our road through life and for which we must be ready to give up all – here and now. The gospels themselves offer lovely examples that match the story of the treasure in the field and the right reaction to the message of the kingdom and the call of Christ the King: for instance, in the vocation of two sets of brothers, Simon Peter and Andrew, and James and John.

> As Jesus passed along the Sea of Galilee, he saw Simon and his brother Andrew casting a net into the sea – for they were fishermen. And Jesus said to them, 'Follow me and I will make you fishers of people.' And immediately they left their nets and followed him. As he went a little further, he saw James and his brother John, who were in their boat mending the nets. Immediately he called them; and they left their father Zebedee in the boat with the hired men, and followed him. (Mark 1:16–18)

The two sets of brothers give us a wonderful instance of what the parable of the treasure in the field can mean to individuals. They have come across someone of immeasurable, incalculable worth, Jesus himself, or rather he has come across them. Suddenly, Peter, Andrew, James and John are offered a magnificent treasure. It is totally free; they do not have to work for it. Like the man who comes across the hidden treasure, the two sets of brothers run into something, or rather Someone, who changes their whole world for them. Of course, they have to give up much if they are going to gain the treasure. The man in the parable sells everything he has to buy the field and win the treasure. Peter, Andrew, James and John must leave behind their boats, their fishing nets and their families if they are going to gain the priceless treasure, which is Jesus himself. Finding a treasure like that is a godsend which turns up once in a lifetime, if that. Coming across the hidden hoard of gold gives the man in the parable a chance that may never come his way again. He has to trust his quick judgement: he must take advantage at once of his opportunity. Jesus is the incredible godsend for Peter, Andrew, James and John; a chance has turned up that may never come again.

They must trust their judgement and risk all to follow Jesus. He is worth gaining at any cost, and will bring them wonderful, lasting joy in the final kingdom of God. Such a chance of a lifetime rules out any half measures and any delay.

Those who come across the treasure will remember the time and place for the rest of their lives. At the birth of Christianity two sets of brothers found their treasure when they were at their work as fishermen by the Sea of Galilee. Many centuries later Paul Claudel, a French writer and diplomat, cherished the moment during the singing of the office in the Cathedral of Notre Dame in Paris when his heart was touched and he believed. It was Christmas Day 1886, and in the crowded congregation he was standing near the second pillar, at the entrance to the choir, on the right, and at the side of the sacristy. It was a moment of light and conversion that Claudel located very precisely and remembered for ever. He came across the treasure of the kingdom at that time and in that place. No one could ever forget such a moment of discovery.

JESUS AND HIS CLAIMS

In his preaching Jesus transposes the parable of the treasure into the peremptory claims he makes on those who respond favourably to the call of the kingdom but are not yet inclined to take instant action. We read in Luke 9:

> To another Jesus said, 'Follow me.' But he said, 'Lord, first let me go and bury my father.' But Jesus said to him, 'Let the dead bury their own dead. But as for you, go and proclaim the kingdom of God.' Another said, 'I will follow you, Lord, but let me first say goodbye to those at my home.' Jesus said to him. 'No one who puts his hand to the plough and looks back is fit for the kingdom of God.' (Luke 9:59–62)

Obedience to the call and gift of the kingdom must take precedence over everything else. Jesus spells out here what finding the treasure could entail. One must instantly decide to sell all that one has and at once secure the amazing gift of the kingdom. Not even the most sacred family ties and duties can stand in the way. If the coming kingdom of God has incalculable value, it costs those who accept it nothing less than everything.

Jesus himself is the kingdom in person, both the present *and the future kingdom.* Deciding for or against God's kingdom means deciding for or against Jesus. He is the treasure hidden in the field, someone who is immeasurably valuable and who can turn our lives around now and for ever. He is the unique godsend from whom we will receive everything if we are ready to lose everything. At the conclusion of the homily at his inaugural Mass in April 2005, Benedict XVI did not mention the parable of the hidden treasure. But he certainly presented Jesus as a unique godsend. The Pope said:

> If we let Christ into our lives we lose nothing, absolutely nothing of what makes life free, beautiful, and good. Do not be afraid of Christ. He takes nothing away, and he gives us everything. When we give ourselves to him, we receive a hundredfold in return. Yes, open, open wide the doors to Christ and you will find true life. Amen.

We rightly interpret the parable in terms of our relationship to the person of Jesus. We may also see the parable as autobiographical, yet another expression of what Jesus himself has based his life upon. For him God's will and the task of bringing the divine kingdom are the treasure in the field. He has said farewell to those at home, and never looks back. He gives his all to the task of proclaiming the kingdom. He has found God's kingdom; he lives for it and makes it accessible for others. He sacrifices everything for this task. At the end it will bring him to a violent death, because he has given his heart to the divine kingdom and his utterly precious mission for us.

At the beginning of this chapter, I explained the petition 'May your kingdom come' as meaning 'come, loving Father, and rule fully as king'. When a king rules, he is in charge and his subjects are expected to do his will. Hence the next petition in the Lord's Prayer follows on naturally: 'may your will be done on earth as in heaven.'

Chapter 7

♦

'MAY YOUR WILL BE DONE, ON EARTH AS IN HEAVEN'

THE THIRD AND FINAL 'you' petition appeals to God to bring it about that the divine will be accomplished on earth in the way it is in heaven. The first two petitions, directly concerned with God's name being made holy and his kingdom coming, respectively, also challenge human beings to let their conduct be changed. But the third petition, about God's will being done '*on earth*, as in heaven', carries even more massive implications for our conduct here and now in this life on earth, before God calls us home through death to our final place 'in heaven'. In that sense it is a bridge petition, which leads on to the 'we' petitions which follow.

This petition entails then a call to surrender our lives to God's loving will and plan for us. It expresses a desire that nothing except the present and future kingdom of God shall determine and rule all our actions and our entire life. In this context those familiar with the Spiritual Exercises of Ignatius Loyola could readily remember the very first 'annotation' or preliminary observation that proposes 'seeking and finding the will of God' and so 'disposing of our life for the salvation of our soul'. What Ignatius primarily (but not exclusively) has in mind is some decision that will shape our lives for ever. But the Spiritual Exercises also envision those who, having sought and found the will of God, have 'disposed of their lives'

74

accordingly. For them the will of God requires faithful obedience – right through the boredom, difficulties, chaos and wear and tear of life. In several parables about faithful waiting, Jesus fills out what doing and continuing to do the divine will looks like. He underlines the need for his followers to show vigilance and faithfulness as they wait for the end. Let us look at three parables gathered in Luke 12 which inculcate this message.

THE WATCHFUL SERVANTS

In the first parable Jesus exploits the image of a great household and its master who is out for the night:

> 'Be dressed for action and have your lamps lit; be like those who are waiting for their master to return from a wedding banquet, so that they may open the door to him as soon as he comes and knocks. Blessed are those servants whom the master finds awake when he comes. Amen, I say to you, he will fasten his belt and have them sit down to eat; and he will come and serve them. If he comes in the middle of the night, or near dawn, and finds them so, blessed are those servants.' (Luke 12:35–38)

Undoubtedly Jesus had first heard of and then seen for himself such households. Did he know people who worked in such households, or had he even himself worked at times for such households? During his ministry we find Jesus a guest of some wealthy householders (e.g. Luke 7:36–50; 19:1–10). Whether or not he enjoyed many personal connections with such great households, they caught his imagination and provided material for some of his parables.

The parable we are looking at resembles somewhat that of the wise and foolish bridesmaids (Matt. 25:1–13). Both stories feature a wedding, people waiting for a central figure who is currently absent but certain to arrive, and the need for lamps to be kept alight. Both stories turn on the fact that the precise time of the arrival – in the first case, of the master, and in the second, of the bridegroom – is not known in advance. They could turn up at any time; no one knows exactly when. But then the differences between the two stories set in. The parable from Matthew specifies a particular number of young women, ten bridesmaids, whereas our parable from Luke includes an indefinite number of servants, who include men and women. These servants are expected to stay awake and not fall asleep, as *all* of the bridesmaids do. In that story the wise bridesmaids doze off along with the foolish ones; their advantage consists not in staying awake but in having a good supply of oil, which the others lack.

Further, Matthew's story initially stations all the brides-maids outside; they are meant to join the procession when the bridegroom fetches his bride from her parents' home. Five of the bridesmaids fail to make the rendezvous and so miss the procession. They have slipped away to buy some oil from dealers (who apparently keep long trading hours). Hence they turn up late and are not admitted when they knock on the door of the bridegroom's house. In Luke's parable, however, the servants are all inside, and should be ready at any moment to open the door and serve a meal. They are waiting for their master to come home from a wedding banquet, not for a bridegroom to arrive. It is the master himself who will come back when he wants to, and will knock at the door of his own house, not five foolish bridesmaids who will knock at someone else's door when they arrive too late.

In Luke's story of the servants waiting at home, they are expected to carry out faithfully their normal duties. They are not given extraordinary commissions, like the three servants in the parable of the talents who receive very large amounts of money for trading or at least investment purposes (Matt. 25:14–30). The expectations are the customary ones when their master is away briefly – perhaps only out for the night – at a banquet. Up and dressed for action, his servants should keep their lamps lit and have food ready for their master when he returns and may want to eat. The last item seems puzzling. Hasn't he been at a banquet? In that Mediterranean culture it would have been considered shameful not to feed guests very well, in fact to over-feed them. Why would the master want to eat? Surely his first thought on returning at midnight or towards dawn would be to head for bed and enjoy some good hours of sleep? Or perhaps we are meant to think that the wedding and subsequent banquet took place at some distance – a day's journey away. But this puzzle pales into insignificance when we read on.

If the servants have been vigilantly ready for the master's return, he will turn around and, even though it is late at night, will offer them a meal at which he himself will serve at table. In an amazing reversal of roles, this wealthy master will not only put on a banquet for his staff but will also take over the job of waiter. Any thought is forgotten of his being tired when he returns late at night from the wedding to which he was invited.

The parable of the watchful and faithful servants ends with a surprise meal for them – a closing detail that summons up the final banquet for all in the coming kingdom of God, a theme which surfaces here and there in the preaching and teaching of Jesus (e.g. Luke 13:29; 22:16) and not least in the story of the prodigal son. The father holds a feast of joy and thanksgiving to celebrate the new life at which his sinful younger son has arrived. The prodigal has shown at least a minimum of fidelity by finally trudging home (Luke 15:11–32).

In the Lord's Prayer we pray, 'May your kingdom come, may your will be done, on earth as in heaven.' We might make things more specific: 'May the banquet of your kingdom come for those who show at least some vigilant fidelity in doing your will.' The master's astonishing gesture in providing a late-night banquet for all his vigilant servants directs our gaze forward – to what will come in the glorious completion of God's reign. The best is yet to be. The main perspective in the parable of the watchful servants (as in the Lord's Prayer itself) is the final revelation of the glorious Christ and the shape of things to come for everybody at the end of all history. Nevertheless, this frame of mind does not exclude post-death expectations for the individual. In fact, Luke encourages his readers to include that perspective by attaching to the story of the watchful servants two further passages which encourage vigilant obedience, but which do so by appealing to two *individual* figures: an owner of a house alert to the possibility of burglary, and a 'faithful and prudent manager'.

THE WATCHFUL HOUSEHOLDER

Luke reports Jesus' words about a watchful householder. 'But know this: if the owner of a house had known at what hour the thief was coming, he would not have let his house be broken into. You also must be ready, for the Son of Man is coming at an unexpected hour' (Luke 12:39–40). Here, obviously, the warning has nothing to do with a delay in a robber's arrival. In the story of the watchful servants, as in the case of the wise and foolish bridesmaids, someone is absent but will *certainly* turn up, even if his arrival may be considerably delayed. In the case of the watchful householder, word has got around about burglaries taking place in the neighbourhood. Are we to imagine a situation that can occur today in a large town? All the other houses on the street have been 'done'. When will they come to break into mine? Yet no one can be certain that the prowling robbers will try to break into every house in the vicinity, even less into this particular one. Perhaps a householder might feel quite convinced that his home will be broken into, because the robbers have hit every other house in the village and they have a reputation for being 'thorough'. Even so, he would still not know the day, let alone the hour, when the robbers will arrive. A wise householder must be constantly watchful in guarding his house against a possible break-in. He should also keep in mind that smart burglars may very well come right at a time when we least expect them.

This kind of story might encourage us to give Jesus, the Son of Man, the title of 'the Smart Burglar', rather than stick with the traditional phrase about 'a thief in the night' (1 Thess. 5:2). Whatever we prefer, Jesus warns us in this parable of vigilance that his coming will be unexpected. It will be unexpected when he comes to end human history and complete the glorious reign of God. It is persistently unexpected when he comes at the end of individual lives. Occasionally doctors and nurses can help friends and relatives anticipate that some very sick person will slip away to God today or tomorrow. Yet even with those who are obviously dying the precise timing of death very often has something surprising about it. Quite regularly we have to say, 'the Son of Man came at an unexpected hour'. In all cases the parable of the watchful householder highlights the need for vigilant fidelity and obedience to the will of God as our lives unfold and move towards an end that is certain but has no precise timing.

THE FAITHFUL MANAGER

Luke links a third story to the parable of the watchful servants: that of a trusty and sensible manager.

> The Lord said, 'Who then is the faithful and prudent manager whom his master will put in charge of his servants, to give them their allowance of food at the proper time? Blessed is that servant whom his master will find at work when he arrives. Truly I tell you, he will put that one in charge of all his possessions. But if that servant says to himself, "My master is delayed in coming", and begins to beat the other servants, men and women, and to eat and drink and get drunk, the master of that servant will come on a day when he does not expect him and at

an hour that he does not know, and will cut him to pieces, and put him with the unfaithful.' (Luke 12:42–46)

With this story we leave the image of a householder and return to that of servants or even slaves. But this time Jesus does not look at those domestics as a group who must be dressed for action and about their duties. He focuses rather on an individual, a manager whom a master has put in charge while he goes off somewhere for some unspecified purpose and also for an unspecified amount of time. This individual, so far from receiving such a dramatic responsibility as that of investing bags of gold for his absent master, is simply expected to carry out the normal duties, like that of providing a regular amount of food for the other servants at the usual times.

But the consequences for the manager are startling. If he behaves in a faithful and sensible way, he will receive a remarkable promotion: he will be put in charge of all his master's possessions. But if he has abused his power and proved arrogant, he will be 'cut to pieces' and 'put with the unfaithful'. One flinches at these words which conclude the parable. With this threat of being torn asunder, we seem to stare into the face of irrational cruelty. Some scholars interpret being 'cut to pieces' as being 'punished severely'. Even so, being 'put with the unfaithful' may seem excessive. Why not simply demote the unfaithful manager, keep him within the establishment, and have him do penance for his irresponsible behaviour? Surely he could be ordered to serve time by working with the lowest ranks of servants or even with the slaves?

The alternatives Jesus proposes are stark – either being put in charge of everything or being 'cut to pieces'. But he certainly wants to underline the need for vigilant and serious fidelity in doing the divine will on earth as our end draws near and hopefully we are granted a place 'in heaven'. The parable of the watchful servants describes the amazing generosity of the master who finds his servants waiting for him when he returns from a wedding. These servants will all be blessed in a remarkable fashion. But what if they have failed to wait up and keep their lamps lit? The parable with which we began this chapter does not spell out the consequences of such a failure. As Luke the evangelist realised, the story of the watchful servants needs to be filled out by the story of the watchful householder and that of the faithful manager.

All three parables press the call to vigilant responsibility, reaching a crescendo with the third. Names play their role in producing this crescendo of seriousness about steady fidelity in doing God's will. The watchful servants wait for their 'master (*kyrios*)' to return. The second parable, that of the watchful householder, emphasises the disciples' need to be always ready for the unpredictable and unexpected return of the 'Son of Man', who will bring the final reign of God. Luke puts the third parable in the mouth of 'the Lord (*ho Kyrios*)', who indicates how he will judge his servants and followers for their fidelity or infidelity. We are dealing with the one life and the one death we face, matters of vital importance. The crucial issue of our fate and the need for vigilant fidelity drew these three utterly serious parables from Jesus.

The faithful waiting Jesus wanted translates for our lives much of what is indicated by the prayer, 'may your will he done, on earth as in heaven'. In a wonderful prayer for fidelity, John Henry Newman helps us to recognise that it is only divine grace that will enable us to stay utterly faithful in doing God's will: 'O Lord, support us all the day long, until the shadows lengthen and the evening comes, and the busy world is hushed, and the fever of life is over, and our work is done. Then in thy mercy grant us a safe lodging, and a holy rest, and peace at the last.'

With this chapter we have completed the 'you' petitions of the Lord's Prayer, those petitions which cry out for the coming of the kingdom of God. We move now to the 'we' petitions, which highlight more the here and now of today: our bread, our debts, the tests we face, and our being menaced by evil.

Part 3

◆

THE 'WE' PETITIONS

Chapter 8

◆

'GIVE US TODAY OUR DAILY BREAD'

U P TO NOW THIS BOOK has been reflecting on the 'you' petitions, the ones which we address to our loving Father and which highlight the coming of the full reign of God. Now we reach the 'we' petitions, in which we turn to ourselves and our needs in the here and now. We do have our needs and problems, sometimes overwhelming needs and desperate problems. In the first of the 'we' petitions Jesus encourages *us* to ask God in a simple and trusting way for *our* needs. Our God, Jesus assures us, takes a highly personal interest in each of us. He is the Father whose attentive love goes far beyond that of normal, caring parents:

> 'Is there anyone among you who, if your child asks for bread, will give him a stone? Or if the child asks for fish, will give him a snake? If you then, who are evil, know how to give good gifts to your children, how much more will your Father in heaven give good things to those who ask him!' (Matt. 7:9–11 par.)

PETITIONARY PRAYER

The 'Give us' of 'Give us today our daily bread' recalls the injunction of Jesus to ask, seek and knock (Matt. 7:7–8 par.).

Jesus certainly endorsed petitionary prayer. His words about God responding to our asking, seeking and knocking seem to come right out of his own experience. Petitions were part of his own life of prayer, and he wanted his followers to pray that way too.

It is important to note that Jesus does not say that 'it will be given to us at once'. Nor does he say that those who seek 'will find immediately', nor that the door will be opened without delay to those who knock. As Tom Casey has observed, 'because we receive time piece by piece, moment by moment', we know or think we know that 'something is right for us today', but cannot always tell 'whether it will be beneficial for us tomorrow'. Hence 'we must trust that God, who possesses time completely, acts in our best interests when he does not answer our prayer in the present'. Casey predicts that 'the day will come when we will feel deep gratitude to him for denying us in the past. God may be giving us something marvellous in the long term by apparently not answering our prayers now.'[1]

When telling us to ask, seek and knock, Jesus does not specify what it is that we might be asking for and seeking, nor does he guarantee when our request might be answered. In his comparison with earthly parents, they answer their children's demand for food by providing bread and fish, two items in the basic diet of those who lived near the shores of Lake Galilee in first-century Palestine. Parents respond to such requests on a daily basis, and do not put off their children by promising that they will give them something to eat tomorrow or next week.

But what is the 'bread' to be prayed for in the 'Our Father'? When do we expect God to provide it? Day by day? Or only at some heavenly banquet to come (Matt. 8:11)?

OUR BREAD. BUT WHEN?

Many have understood the bread-petition against the background of two experiences: the Exodus experience and the experience of Jesus' own preaching. In this view he invites his disciples to ask day by day for the food which they need. They should trust that God will provide them with food each day, just as he fed the Israelites in the desert with the manna which they gathered. Jesus himself has talked elsewhere about trusting God to provide for ordinary human needs (Matt. 6:25–34 par.). In these terms we pray together for the bread that we constantly need to sustain life and support human existence and relationships day by day. In his version of the Lord's Prayer, Luke, by proposing prayer for bread 'each day' instead of Matthew's 'today', may be a better guide to what Jesus originally intended. Luke's version strengthens the case for praying day by day for our basic needs.

Matthew's version of the Lord's Prayer opens up, however, a second possibility by applying to 'bread' a very rare and obscure Greek word, *epiousios*;[2] it has normally been translated as 'daily', but it could mean 'for tomorrow'. That 'tomorrow' could even be 'the great tomorrow' or definitive age of salvation to begin with the final coming of Christ in judgement. The vivid expectations of the end, which Christ and his followers fostered (see Chapter 6 above), could lend credence to this interpretation. Hence the petition might be: 'Give us the bread for the great tomorrow, the heavenly banquet to come with the final age.'

A third, perhaps more convincing, possibility opts for an 'already' and a 'not yet'. Thus the petition would be: 'Give us already today our bread which we expect at the great tomorrow but which has not yet arrived.' We can put this more briefly: 'Our bread for tomorrow give us today.' Thus the bread that we eat day by day would anticipate and make present now the bread of the heavenly banquet that is still to come.

This third explanation bears with it two important impli-cations. First, the bread of the great tomorrow will be shared; no one will dine alone at the banquet of all nations (Matt. 8:11). Anticipating that bread now, we must share it and eat together. Second, to pray that way is to introduce overtones of Jesus as the Bread of Life, with whom we will be united in the glorious life to come. Christ is the Bread of Life in two senses: he is the Word of God that we hear and the Bread of the Eucharist that we feed from here and now, in anticipation of our definitive union with Christ in the world to come. An Anglo-Saxon expansion of this petition in the Lord's Prayer takes us in this direction: 'Give us now today, Lord of human beings, High King of the heavens, our bread, which you sent into the world as salvation for the souls of humankind: that is the pure Christ, the Lord God.'[3]

OUR BREAD. BUT WHAT?

In wrestling above with the 'timing' involved in the gift of 'our bread', we had to say something about what that gift is and what it will be. Our normal daily needs? Jesus himself as the Bread of Life? Or both? In the third century, St Cyprian of Carthage understood our 'daily bread' as daily sustenance, but even more as the Eucharist that we require for our spiritual survival.[4] A hundred years later, St Gregory of Nyssa offered a 'material' explanation: our ordinary needs of food, drink and so forth constitute the 'daily bread' for which we pray in the Lord's Prayer.[5] Many centuries later, Martin Luther and John Calvin were to follow the same 'material' line in explaining the petition.

St Augustine of Hippo, however, allowed for both a material and a spiritual account of 'daily bread'. He under-stood the petition to involve both our daily material needs and our daily spiritual bread. Under the latter he included both the Word of God and the Eucharist, Christ in the double perspective of the 'Bread of Life' who sustains us for time and eternity (John 6:25–65): 'We are praying for the needful daily bread for the body, and the consecrated visible Bread, and the invisible bread of the Word of God.'⁶ As regards our 'daily bread', Augustine takes us in the right direction – towards the double sense of the 'Bread of Life' that shapes the discourse in John's gospel which comments on the feeding of the five thousand (John 6:1–71). That gospel does not include the 'Our Father' as such, but various passages parallel, evoke and interpret the petitions of the prayer. In particular, John 6 forms a sustained comment on 'Give us today our daily bread'. Let me illustrate this remark by taking up two films.

SATISFYING THE HUNGRY HEART

Some years ago I switched on the television and caught an instalment in a long-running soap opera. The central star was an attractive wife and mother, a woman in her late thirties. At the end of some domestic ups and downs, she looked off into the distance and asked: 'What's it all about?' A woman friend with her seemed equally puzzled about the meaning of it all, and replied: 'You tell me.' Well, what *is* it all about? At times it feels as if we cannot make sense of our lot, and it all feels like the ache of a never-satisfied hunger.

In Franco Zeffirelli's film *Jesus of Nazareth*, one of the most powerful points in the whole film comes when he links the feeding of the five thousand (John 6:1–14) to the conversion of Mary Magdalene.⁷ A wonderful camera shot picks her out in the large crowd. She bites on a chunk of bread and bursts into tears of joy and repentance. With her hands gripping the bread, she fixes her tear-filled eyes on Jesus. She knows that her hungry heart has finally found the One who promises, 'Those who come to me shall not hunger. Those who believe in me shall never thirst' (John 6:35). The scene matches perfectly that line from the 1976 prize-winning hymn, 'You satisfy the hungry heart'.

What can we say about the hungers of the human heart that

Christ, the Bread of Life, satisfies? We might describe them in various ways. But they seem to come down to three things: a deep desire for life, for meaning and for love. We hunger and thirst to live and to live fully. Second, we want things to make sense. When our goals are clear and the meaning of things comes through brightly, we can cope with great, even immense, difficulties. Absurd situations leave us floating aimlessly and without a compass. Third, we hunger to love and be loved. William Blake (1757–1827) put it this way: where love is concerned, our hearts are a 'bottomless gorge'. To sum up, we crave for a life that is absolutely full and will never end. We search for a meaning that will light up everything. We hunger for the perfect love that will be utterly and enduringly satisfying.

Zeffirelli's picture of Mary Magdalene, with a piece of bread at the moment of her conversion, illustrates a great truth of our daily lives. Christ is the One who can completely and finally satisfy all our hungers. And that's what it's all about, and especially when we pray, 'Give us today our daily bread.'

Chapter 9

♦

'FORGIVE US OUR DEBTS, AS WE ALSO HAVE FORGIVEN OUR DEBTORS'

A FEW YEARS AGO I gave myself a refresher course in the OT by watching a whole series of films on biblical characters that had been produced by a joint American-Italian enterprise. The films took me through the stories of Noah, Abraham and Sarah, Jacob and Rachel, Moses, Samson and Delilah, and right on down to the life of King David. If one puzzled over Elizabeth Hurley and her performance as Delilah, some outstanding actors and actresses, like Diana Rigg and Max von Sydow, turned up in the series.

One of the most moving moments in all that viewing came with the ending of the story of the patriarch Joseph. His brothers, who years before had treated him cruelly and sold him into slavery, unexpectedly find themselves alone with the powerful prime minister of Egypt. He is none other than Joseph himself. The camera sweeps from trembling face to trembling face. They cannot bring themselves to believe what they have just heard. After all that they did to him, Joseph has forgiven them and truly loves them. Here the film follows closely the biblical text. Right to the very end of the Joseph cycle in the Book of Genesis, Joseph's brothers are still terrified that he has not truly forgiven them. He may have buried the hatchet for the moment. But he must have carefully marked the spot. Now that their father Jacob is dead, Joseph will dig up the hatchet and finally have his revenge. With tears filling his eyes, Joseph once again assures his brothers that he has truly forgiven them and will always take care of them (Gen. 50:15–21). Both the biblical story of Joseph and, in its own visual way, the American-Italian film about him highlight the great challenge which forgiveness presents.

THREE PRESUPPOSITIONS

The plea for forgiveness in the Lord's Prayer rests on three presuppositions. First, we all have our debts. Paul, before writing in his Letter to the Romans about the forgiveness and redemption that come through Christ, insists that 'all have sinned and are deprived of the glory/beauty of God' (Rom. 3:23). The Apostle knew that we can resist this idea and think of ourselves as essentially innocent. In modern times Albert Camus (1913–60) classically expressed in his novel *The Fall* what he called 'the most natural idea of a human being', that of one's personal innocence. 'We are all like that young Frenchman' who was arrested in the Second World War, arrived at the concentration camp of Buchenwald and insisted on registering a complaint. 'The clerk and his comrades laughed: "Useless old man. You don't lodge complaints here." "But you see, sir," said the little Frenchman, "my case is different. I am innocent!"' As Camus comments drily, 'We are all exceptional cases.'[1] The First Letter of John calls for honesty about our sinful condition and promises forgiveness to those who honestly confess their sins: 'If we say we have no sin, we deceive ourselves, and the truth is not in us. If we confess our sins, he who is faithful and just will forgive our sins and cleanse us from all unrighteousness' (1 John 1:8–9).

Then a second presupposition lies behind the petition for forgiveness. There is *no self-forgiveness*, since sin involves not only damage to ourselves but also (and even more) some kind of breakdown in our personal relationship with God and usually with one another. In the proper sense of the word, we

92

cannot forgive ourselves. Nor can we by ourselves repair the results of our sins. Left to our own resources, we remain incapable of healing the harm our sins cause. In the Lord's Prayer, Jesus is not proposing a self-help spirituality, as if self-acceptance would fix everything up. He does not say, 'forgive others and then you will be at peace' or 'forget about how others have offended you and your mind will become serene again'. Rather, we are to ask our gracious God to forgive our sins and to do so in view of the fact that we are ready to forgive the sins others may have committed against us.

Third, the Lord's Prayer implies a solidarity in seeking, accepting and expressing forgiveness. To be sure, Jesus strikes a different note in such parables as that of the prodigal son and that of the Pharisee and the publican. Here individuals confess their sinfulness and ask for forgiveness. Then we have individuals, like the woman who was a sinner (Luke 7:36–50) and Zacchaeus (Luke 19:1–10), who are forgiven by Jesus, even though they do not explicitly confess their sins and ask for forgiveness. But in the 'Our Father' the plea for forgiveness comes from the group: 'forgive us our debts'. What Jesus proposes here matches his plea that those who hear him will follow the example of the Ninevites. They collectively repented at the preaching of Jonah (Luke 11:29–32 par.). At various times in the OT, especially at the time of the Babylonian captivity, the prophets and psalmists express collective repentance and ask to be forgiven and restored. A haunting Lenten antiphon serves to sum up this familiar OT theme: 'pay heed, O Lord and forgive [us], for we have sinned against you (*attende, Domine, et miserere, quia peccavimus tibi*).'

In the sacrament of reconciliation, the prayer of absolution matches the major emphasis of the Lord's Prayer by first invoking collective forgiveness before moving to the forgiveness of the individual penitent. 'God, the Father of mercies, through the death and resurrection of his Son has reconciled the world to himself and sent the Holy Spirit among us for the forgiveness of sins. Through the ministry of

93

the Church may God give you pardon and peace, and I absolve you from your sins in the name of the Father, and of the Son, and of the Holy Spirit.'

SINNERS, DEBTORS AND FORGIVENESS

In both classical and (later) Hellenistic Greek, the words for 'debts' and 'debtors' retained their secular reference and were not used metaphorically in a religious context for sin and sinners. On the contrary, the equivalent Aramaic word was so used. Matthew, even though writing in Greek, maintains the original (Aramaic) expression used by Jesus: 'forgive us our debts, as we also have forgiven our debtors'. Luke (or the tradition on which he draws), to make things more immediately intelligible to Christians of a Gentile background, substitutes 'sins' – at least in the first part of the petition: 'forgive us our sins, as we ourselves forgive everyone in debt to us' (Luke 11:4).[2]

More importantly, Luke's form of the Lord's Prayer, even if shorter, does not fail to include the plea for forgiveness and the condition for receiving this – both essential points in Jesus' programme for the kingdom: 'forgive us our sins, as we ourselves forgive everyone in debt to us.' Nothing shows more clearly God's merciful love towards us than the divine forgiveness. Nothing shows more clearly our love towards others than our willingness to forgive others from our heart. This is the one point in the 'Our Father' where Jesus expects us to testify before God what we are doing. He does not ask us to pray: 'Give us this day our daily bread, as we give their daily bread to others', or, 'do not bring us into temptation, just as we do not bring others into temptation'. The only point which calls for personal testimony about our attitudes and 'performance' is forgiveness: 'forgive us our debts, as we also have forgiven our debtors.'

The parable of the unmerciful servant (Matt. 18:23–35) puts into relief God's greatness and our littleness. Over against the mind-boggling debt owed to the king, £2,250,000,000 or nearly 4 billion US dollars, anything that might be owed to us is as small as the debt owed to the unmerciful servant, £6,000 or US$9,000. The parable brings out the magnitude of God's prior forgiveness towards us, and its consequence: we must forgive in our turn. The Lord's Prayer represents the need to grant forgiveness to others as a condition for receiving God's forgiveness. The divine forgiveness cannot be expected, if we have withheld our forgiveness from other human beings. Or, to put it in a more accurate way, our forgiveness of one another shows how far we have accepted God's forgiveness and have let it change our lives.

THE DIFFICULTY OF FORGIVENESS

Matthew seems to have realised how difficult it is for us to forgive others. Hence, immediately after the Lord's Prayer he inserts an exhortation by Jesus on the importance of forgiveness: 'if you forgive others their trespasses, your heavenly Father will also forgive you. But if you do not forgive others, neither will your Father forgive your trespasses' (Matt. 6:14–15). The evangelist could have inserted this exhortation elsewhere in the Sermon on the Mount. Or he could have chosen a different piece of teaching to drive home another petition in the Lord's Prayer: for instance, the closing plea to 'deliver us from the evil one'. Thus he might have inserted here a warning from Jesus that turns up four chapters later: 'Do not be afraid of those who kill the body but cannot kill the soul. Rather, be afraid of the one who can destroy both body and soul in hell' (Matt. 10:28). But by adding this exhortation on forgiveness right after the Lord's Prayer, Matthew drives home the importance and difficulty of forgiving one another.

As I write these pages, the centenary celebrations for the birth of Jean-Paul Sartre are in full blast. In one of his novels he caricatures a happy character who could see no difficulty about forgiveness. He believed that the only thing needed to settle all conflicts was a little common sense. If only it were as easy as that! Our world desperately needs forgiveness between entire nations and large groups, who continue to savage and kill each other with irrational ferocity. But we cannot expect forgiveness on a grand scale between peoples and races, if we fail to practise it on a small scale in our own lives.

G. K. Chesterton once remarked, 'I find it easy to love Eskimos, because I have never seen an Eskimo. But I find it hard to love my neighbour who plays the piano over my head too late at night.' We all have something to forgive in others, perhaps much to forgive, and it will not be as trifling as someone on the floor above us who plays the piano or listens to the stereo into the night. It may be our parents who need our forgiveness. It could be someone who has persistently treated us as if we were a thing and not a person. It may be that friends, colleagues or even close relatives have betrayed us or at least let us down very badly. Forgiveness is generally difficult and costly.

I think here of an Anglican bishop in Northern Uganda, whose wife was killed by a landmine in 1997. In his diocese nearly all of the eighty places for worship were destroyed, damaged or had to be abandoned because of mindless terrorist activity. Far from indulging bitter anger over his tragic losses, the bishop went on working to bring peace and forgiveness to his tormented country. Over the last ten years, another African has delivered to me the same message, almost day by day. Very often I take breakfast with a tall, Tutsi priest, many of whose close relatives and friends were hacked to death in the genocidal massacres of 1994. His gentle, compassionate attitude constantly makes me think: 'How can I dare to think that someone has treated me badly, when Theo shows such loving forgiveness?'

Living in Rome through the late 1970s and into the early 1980s made me sadly conscious of the senseless and cruel killings carried out by members of the Red Brigade and other terrorist organisations. At the same time, the funeral services of their victims over and over again revealed the power God gave to grief-stricken people to forgive and show mercy. In May 1980 Walter Tobagi, a young journalist, was assassinated by the Red Brigade in revenge for what he had written against them. At the funeral Archbishop (later Cardinal) Carlo Maria Martini of Milan spoke of a 'mystery of meaninglessness and madness'. But then he reminded his congregation of the great certainty that Jesus brings: 'What is meaningless can gain a meaning.' The prayers of the faithful which followed the Archbishop's homily showed most movingly how Jesus can help those in terrible sorrow to see meaning in what they experience and to express forgiveness and love. Stella Tobagi, left widowed with her two little children, had written this prayer and sat with her arms around her son and daughter, while her sister read it:

> Lord, we pray for those who killed Walter, and for all people who wrongly hold that violence is the only way for resolving problems. May the power of your Spirit change the hearts of men, and out of Walter's death may there be born a hope which the force of arms will never be able to defeat.

Stella Tobagi, no less than the Ugandan bishop and the Tutsi priest, showed us a follower of Jesus who forgives from the heart.

GIVING AND FORGIVING

None of these great Christians would pretend that forgiveness is easy. In their own way some modern languages make this very point. To 'forgive', like the French *pardonner*, the German *vergeben*, the Italian *perdonare* and the Spanish *perdonar*, is a longer and strengthened form of the verb 'give'. It sounds as though 'forgiving' is giving to the power of 'n', in fact until seventy times seven times, as Jesus himself put it (Matt. 18:21–22). To give to others is not always easy; to forgive them can be much harder, even heroic. Jesus has sometimes been described as 'the man born to give'. He could be described even better as 'the man born to forgive'. Those who see the highpoint of his parables, other teaching and whole ministry as loving mercy, forgiveness and reconciliation argue a good case.

Jesus struck his contemporary critics as scandalous in a number of things he said and did. Nowhere did they see him more scandalously generous than in his readiness to forgive. Here they found him dangerously permissive. But, if there is going to be any area where love should make us 'permissive', it is in this matter of forgiving others. Jesus showed himself the utter opposite of the unmerciful servant (Matt. 18:23–35). We should be horrified even to imagine him seizing someone by the throat and instantly demanding his rights. He was patient and magnanimous to the extreme. He has left us the challenge of following him in his way of forgiveness.

At this point we move beyond the first two 'we' petitions. They are very basic pleas – to feed our hunger and forgive our sins. Now we turn to deliverance from (overwhelming) temptation and from evil.

Chapter 10

♦

'DO NOT BRING US INTO TEMPTATION'

Fʀᴏᴍ ᴛʜᴇ sᴛᴀʀᴛ Cʜʀɪsᴛɪᴀɴs have struggled with this petition, and it has probably prompted more theological comment than any other section of the Lord's Prayer. In the early third century Tertullian proposed 'Do not suffer (*ne patiaris*) us to be led into temptation'. A few decades later his fellow African, St Cyprian of Carthage, followed the lead of Tertullian and endorsed this version. More than a century later St Augustine of Hippo, also a North African, knew this tradition, but preferred 'Do not bring (*ne auferas*) us into temptation'. In sixteenth-century England King Henry VIII followed Tertullian's lead and imposed 'Suffer us not to be led' in the 1538 *Primer*. A few years later, in the 1549 Prayer Book, Thomas Cranmer, the Archbishop of Canterbury, endorsed a version that followed the line of Augustine and had spread widely in late medieval England: 'Lead us not'. That has remained the rendering familiar to all English-speaking Christians. Whether we maintain 'Lead us not' or prefer 'Do not suffer us to be led', what does it mean? What are we praying for at this point in the Lord's Prayer?

THE TEMPTATIONS OF JESUS

The noun 'temptation (*peirasmos*)' and the associated verb 'tempt/test (*peirazō*)' turn up here and there in the NT and not least in connection with Jesus.[1] Immediately after his baptism he is driven by the Spirit into the desert, where for forty days he is 'tested by Satan' (Mark 1:13). Mark leaves it all as briefly and simply as that. Matthew and Luke offer much longer versions of that stint in the desert and the temptations involved. They recall even more clearly than Mark the way Israel was tested during forty years in the desert.

Matthew has Jesus 'being tested by the devil', who is also called 'the tempter' and 'Satan' (Matt. 4:1–11). The devil is concerned to probe the identity of Jesus ('If you are the Son of God'). The devil also wants to disturb his sense of mission by raising concerns about his practical needs and safety. Jesus is confronted by personal evil, which is not only actively hostile to God but also wants to usurp the place of God. The devil promises Jesus 'all the kingdoms of the earth and their glory, if you will fall down and worship me'. Jesus refuses with firmness ('you shall worship the Lord your God and serve only him'), and the devil leaves him. In *The Gospel According to St Matthew*, Pier Paolo Pasolini brilliantly pictures the puzzlement of the devil. As he moves away confused and hesitant, Satan's feet disturb the sand and convey a sense of his bewilderment. With whom has he tried his series of temptation?

Luke's account of the temptations (Luke 4:1–13) ends with an ominous hint: 'When the devil had finished every test, he departed from him until an opportune time.' That would come when Jesus faced his arrest and said to those who came to seize him: 'this is your hour and the power of darkness' (Luke 22:53). At the Last Supper he had already acknowledged his disciples to be those 'who have stood by me in my trials (*peirasmoi*)' (Luke 22:28). In the Garden of Gethsemane Jesus warns Peter, James and John about the time of trial they now face: 'watch and pray that you may not come into [suc-cumb to] temptation/trial' (Luke 22:46). They will be shortly faced with a terrifying test at the arrest, passion and death of Jesus.

Some film directors have developed these hints to bring Satan quite blatantly into the story of Jesus' suffering and death. In a 1999 American/Italian film, *Jesus*, the devil appears in the desert as a plausible contemporary crook – a bit overweight, with greasy hair, and wearing an Armani suit. He returns in the same garb during the agony Jesus undergoes in Gethsemane. Mel Gibson's *The Passion of Christ* opens with Jesus' agony in the garden and introduces Satan into the scene. He appears as a loathsome androgynous figure and a menacing snake; he will lurn up again as the androgynous figure in scenes that follow.

Clearly when we pray 'Do not bring us into temptation', we may think especially of Jesus and his being tested by forces actively hostile to God, especially at the beginning of his ministry and at the end of his earthly life. But what about the temptation/testing that we face?

TEMPTATION AND OURSELVES

Some take 'temptation (*peirasmos*)' to denote, in particular, the final crisis of world history, a cosmic, closing battle between good and evil, the kind of final onslaught of evil imaged forth at the end of *The Lord of the Rings*, and by what will come in the *Harry Potter* series. The Book of Revelation anticipates such a finale but does so in the comforting message from the glorious Christ and his Spirit to 'the church of Philadelphia': 'Because you have kept my word of patient endurance, I will keep you from the hour of trial (*peirasmos*) which is coming on the whole world, to try those who dwell upon the earth' (Rev. 3:10). Yet even the Book of Revelation recognises that such 'testing' need not be on a cosmic scale. It applies this language to the suffering of the church of Smyrna when some of its members are arrested and briefly imprisoned (Rev. 2:10). There can be smaller testings, as well as *the* great testing.

The First Letter of Peter, written to encourage Christians who are suffering, observes that God allows believers to endure various 'trials (*peirasmoi*)' to prove and enhance the quality of their faith (1 Pet. 1:6). They are in God's keeping and can rejoice because they will receive salvation, 'the outcome of their faith' (1 Pet. 1:9). The testing need not be on a cosmic scale that involves a final showdown between good and evil.

Hence, even if the 'temptation' intended by 'Do not bring us into temptation' may point emphatically to some final clash between good and evil, a closing test in the last hours of the world, it is not limited to that eschatological crisis. We are living anyway in the 'end-time', and constantly face battles in which we can be tempted to despair and lose faith. We pray that our loving Father will keep up our morale. When 1 Peter writes of 'the fiery ordeal' (1 Pet. 4:12), it probably refers to persecutions. Our fiery ordeals can take many forms: such as the unexpected death of some dear relative or friend, scandals in the Church, and failure in some major project in our life. In the explanation of the parable of the sower, Matthew includes the threat of apostasy. Nowadays, at least in the Western world, such apostasy could be caused not so much by persecution as by steady pressure from a society and culture that are persistently hostile or at least indifferent to faith. These and other dramatic moments of trial fill out what 'temptation' means. In particular, we should pray to be preserved from giving up faith in Christ.

In the Lord's Prayer we pray, in effect, 'Do not let us fall under or succumb to temptation', and not 'deliver us from temptation and suffering'. Our loving 'Abba' is not in the business of taking away every test and trial. Back in the second century Origen made such a comment on the 'Our Father' in his *Treatise on Prayer* (29.90).[2] Tests and temptations are everywhere. The Lord expects us to pray that we not be overcome by temptation, not that we may escape from it. God is an amazing mixture of compassion and strength, and will enable us to withstand any of the trials we have to face. Hence with confidence we can pray, 'Do not let us fall under or succumb to temptation. Protect us and help us to endure our testing.'

My exposition of 'Do not bring us into temptation' has taken shape around the example of Jesus, tested in the desert and in his passion. The explanation of the final 'we' petition in the Lord's Prayer will also take its shape from what he did and what he does for us.

Chapter 11

♦

'BUT DELIVER US FROM THE EVIL ONE'

The Lord's Prayer finishes here with a petition that incorporates a major element in the ministry of Jesus and his preaching of the kingdom: his effective power over demonic forces. His mission as the world's Redeemer has already emerged in the previous three 'we' petitions. Like the opening 'you' petitions, these four petitions are addressed to the Father, but the Son is very much present in them. 'Give us today our daily bread' reminds us of how Christ provides for our needs and feeds us with the Eucharist, thus anticipating the definitive fullness of salvation to come at the end. He forgives our sins, as he repeatedly did during his ministry to the sick and sinful. He strengthens us not to fail in moments when we are shaken and deeply tested. Now 'deliver us' vigorously sounds the note of redemption, already exercised during the ministry of Jesus.

THE MINISTRY OF JESUS

When we turn to the ministry of Jesus, we find vivid examples of what the seventh and last petition of the Lord's Prayer entails. The gospels see human existence as a battlefield dominated by one or another supernatural force: God or Satan. Right from his baptism, we see Jesus struggling with the devil for the control of humanity in what is the end-time of history. The evil one (*ho ponēros*) in Matthew's version of the 'Our Father' is the same 'evil one' who will be mentioned when the parable of the sower is explained. The evil one comes and snatches away 'the word of the kingdom' which is sown in human hearts (Matt. 13:19). But Jesus is 'the stronger one' and strikingly overcomes the demonic powers through his exorcisms (Mark 3:22–27). Jesus enters the 'strong man's house, ties him up and plunders his property' (Mark 3:22–27).

When Jesus empowers the seventy-two for a trial mission and sends them out, they return jubilant and say: 'Lord, even the demons are subject to us because of your name.' Jesus comments on this victory over Satan: 'I saw Satan fall like lightning from heaven' (Luke 10:18). The dominion of Satan is at an end; the dominion of Christ is imposing itself. This victory over the powers of evil will be completed with the coming of the final reign of Christ (Rev. 20:1–6). Shortly after the mission of the seventy-two, Luke reports Jesus as saying: 'If it is by the finger of God that I cast out demons, then the kingdom of God has come to you' (Luke 11:20). The language here echoes what is said about 'the finger of God' empowering Moses and Aaron (Exod. 8:15). God's power worked through those two OT leaders to liberate the people from the slavery of Egypt. In his ministry Jesus exerts this same divine power to liberate people enslaved by demonic forces.

During the ministry of Jesus, at times it happens that someone in the power of evil spirits is present when Jesus is teaching (Mark 1:2–8 parr.). The encounter, which ends with Jesus driving out an evil spirit, can almost seem to have happened by accident. At other times relatives or friends seek Jesus out and implore his help, as does a Syrophoenician woman whose daughter is possessed (Mark 7:24–30 par.). In all cases the power of Jesus is very apparent in the exorcisms. He does not begin by laying on hands, using incantations or appealing in prayer to God for the expulsion of demons. He simply rebukes them, commands them and casts them out. A

Gerasene demoniac provides the classic example of Jesus delivering someone from the power of the evil one, especially in the long, vividly dramatic form supplied by Mark (Mark 5:1–20 parrs.).

THE GERASENE DEMONIAC

Presumably a Gentile, this possessed man has behaved in a violent, antisocial and self-destructive manner. He lives among the tombs, and so already belongs, as it were, to the abode of the dead. He is an outcast, excluded from the community, someone with whom no one dares to live. The people of the neighbouring town do not speak with him, let alone love him. He is one of the living dead, an exiled non-person who is cut off from society, feared and despised. In the words of Mark:

> He lived among the tombs, and no one could restrain him any more, even with a chain. For he had often been restrained with shackles and chains, but the chains he wrenched apart and the shackles he broke in pieces. No one had the strength to subdue him. Night and day among the tombs and on the mountains, he was always howling and bruising himself with stones. (Mark 5:3–5)

But with a word Jesus overcomes those who torment the poor man, the demonic forces who call themselves 'Legion'. These many demons are then deprived of any place to stay in this world. They are given permission to enter a great herd of swine. Then the animals rush at once down the steep bank into the sea and are drowned.

Without being asked to deliver the demoniac, Jesus sets him free, restores his human dignity and reintegrates him into the community of men and women. When people come out of the nearby town, they find the demoniac clothed, in his right mind and peacefully sitting near Jesus. The demons who have tormented the demoniac are gone and have seemingly perished with the pigs; he enjoys peace of mind, and has been led back into the life of human society. The people who have come to see what has happened are no longer terrorised by the former demoniac. But they are 'afraid', and beg Jesus to leave their neighbourhood. Do these Gentiles fear that, after the suicidal stampede of the pigs, they might suffer even further loss of stock? Or is their reaction something deeper, a fear of the numinous power that Jesus has just shown?

The reaction of the ex-demoniac himself is very different. He wants to stay with Jesus. Does he fear a relapse, once Jesus is gone? Or, as seems more likely, has his deliverance from the forces of evil given rise to a desire to follow Jesus as a disciple? Jesus tells him: 'Go home to your own people, and tell them how much the *Lord* has done for you, and what mercy he has shown you.' The man obeys, and begins to 'proclaim in the Decapolis how much *Jesus* had done for him'. The evangelist Mark seems to hint at an equivalence between 'the Lord' and 'Jesus', and clearly presents the ex-demoniac as the first evangelist for Jesus. He proclaims Jesus not simply to his 'own people', but also in the whole Decapolis, a collection of ten cities in eastern Palestine.

ALL EVIL

In many translations the closing petition of the Lord's Prayer has been rendered 'deliver us from evil'. In that case we pray to be liberated from evil in all its shapes and forms: from sin, death and satanic forces. Also in this more global sense, Jesus proves to be our deliverer. The gospels offer a spectacular example in the case of a paralytic (Mark 2:1–12 parr.). He is lowered on a stretcher through a roof and placed on the ground right in front of Jesus. The Lord delivers him first from the evil of sin: 'Son, your sins are forgiven you.' Then he delivers him from his physical suffering: 'Take up your stretcher and walk.' In short, Jesus delivers the man from spiritual and physical evil; he gives him 'health in mind and body' – to quote a prayer said before holy communion by the priest.

The closing petition of the Lord's Prayer should, I think, be translated as 'deliver us from the evil one'. Yet it makes very good sense, if we keep the traditional rendering, 'deliver us from evil'. Either way, we pray that our loving Father will deliver us through the power of Christ and the Holy Spirit.

Obviously the final petitions of the 'Our Father' go closely together: 'Do not bring us into temptation but deliver us from the evil one.' Six years ago I had a vivid experience of what these two petitions could mean in practice. At the Colosseum in Rome, on 7 May 2000, John Paul II led an ecumenical commemoration of the countless witnesses of Christian faith in the twentieth century. Anglicans, Catholics, Orthodox and Protestants from various denominations joined the Pope in remembering with gratitude and admiration those men and women from all parts of the world who had gone through terrible sufferings and often death for their loyalty to Christ. They did not succumb to temptation and were delivered from evil. At the service there were hymns, scripture readings, prayers and testimonials written by or written about these heroes and heroines of faith. These testimonials form a striking, modern commentary on the final two petitions from the Lord's Prayer.

There was a testimony from a Chinese Catholic, Margaret Chou. She was arrested at the age of twenty-two and spent the years from 1958 to 1979 either in prison or in labour camps. She wrote of her experiences:

> In the prison factory we worked eighteen hours a day, seven days a week. The drums would wake us up at four in the morning. Before long, due to extreme fatigue, I lost my appetite. At night, I collapsed on my bed without even washing my face. This routine kept going for a year.

Right at the beginning, however, a kind of deliverance had come in the form of mutual support. Chou explained:

A few days after I arrived at the prison, an officer asked me: 'What is your crime?' I snapped back, 'I did not commit any crime. I was arrested because I was a Catholic and tried to defend my faith.' The officer became very angry and shouted: 'If you did not commit any crime, why are you here?' I was stunned by his extreme anger and shut up. The whole factory was dead silent.

Because of this incident, Chou added:

I discovered several Catholics. We quickly united. Among them was a girl named Tsou. She was especially good to me. Unfortunately, after four years she broke down mentally. The officer even used her mental condition as a violation of prison regulations. They tied her up. They hung her up and beat her. They extended her sentence twice. Although she has now completed her time, she is still in the labour camp [and] without proper care.

After China, we heard a testimony from Melanesia. On 2 September 1942 Philip Strong, the Anglican Bishop of Papua New Guinea, was interned in a prison camp together with eight of his priests and two lay persons. He had refused to leave his diocese, even though enemy forces were closing in fast on the country. Shortly before his arrest, he wrote to his clergy:

I have, from the first, felt that we must endeavour to carry on our work in all circumstances, no matter what the cost may be to us individually. God expects this of us. The Church at home, which sent us out, will surely expect it of us ... The people whom we serve expect it of us.

Bishop Strong concluded by evoking what happened in the Garden of Gethsemane: 'We could never hold up our heads again, if, for our own sake, we all forsook him [Christ] and fled when the shadows of his passion began to gather around him in his spiritual body, the church in Papua.'

On that May afternoon in the year 2000 at the Colosseum we also listened to testimonies about and from witnesses to the faith in Africa and Latin America, as well as from those who suffered under Nazism and Communism in Europe. We heard the stories of Christians like the German Paul Schneider and the Albanian Anton Luli. These testimonies revealed the power that comes from God our Father preserving believers under trial and delivering them from evil. Paul Schneider, a Lutheran pastor, who was born in 1897, became a member of the circle of pastors founded by Martin Niemöller. He was arrested and taken to Buchenwald in 1937 because of his opposition to Nazism. In the concentration camp he was mistreated and tortured, because he refused to pay homage to Hitler's swastika. In April 1938, he was put in solitary confinement in the camp's bunker, and it was here he spent the last fourteen months of his life. He died on 18 July 1939, as a result of torture and 'medical' experimentation. An Austrian Catholic priest, who was also imprisoned in Buchenwald but survived, had this to say about Paul Schneider:

> In front of the single-storeyed building of the camp, there stretched the immense parade ground. On feast days, in the silence of the roll-call, suddenly from behind the dark bars of the bunker, there echoed the powerful voice of Pastor Schneider. He would preach like a prophet, or rather he would start to preach.

The Austrian priest explained why the sermons from the bunker were cut short:

> On Easter Sunday, for instance, we heard to our surprise the powerful words: 'Thus says the Lord: I am the resurrection and the life!' The long lines of prisoners stood at attention, deeply moved by the courage and energy of that indomitable will ... He could never utter more than a few phrases. Then we would hear raining down on him the blows from the guards' truncheons.

Father Anton Luli, a Jesuit priest, was born in Albania in 1910. During the Communist regime, he was imprisoned for seventeen years, followed by eleven years of forced labour. Finally, he was released in late 1989, and could publicly exercise his priestly ministry until he died in 1998. Before he died, he had spoken to an assembly of bishops in Rome. That testimony was read out during the service at the Colosseum in 2000:

> I learned what freedom is at eighty years of age, when I was able to celebrate my first Mass with the people. The years spent in prison were truly terrible. During my first month, on the night of Christmas, they made me strip and then hung me from the rafters with a rope, so that I could touch the ground only with the tip of my toes. It was cold. I felt an icy chill moving up my body. It was as though I were slowly dying. When the freezing cold was about to arrive at my chest, I let out a desperate cry. My torturers ran to me; they kicked me mercilessly, and then they took me down.

Luli added:

> They often tortured me with electricity, putting two electrodes in my ears. It was an indescribably horrible experience. That I remained alive is a miracle of God's grace. I bless the Lord who gave me, his poor and weak minister, the grace to remain faithful to him in a life lived almost entirely in chains. Many of my confreres died as martyrs; it was my lot, however, to remain alive, in order to bear witness.

These testimonials from or about Margaret Chou, Philip Strong, Paul Schneider, Anton Luli and others, which we heard that day in 2000 at the Colosseum, were followed by the singing of the Lord's Prayer and a closing blessing from Pope John Paul II. The testimonials filled out marvellously what it might mean when we pray, 'Do not bring us into temptation

111

but deliver us from the evil one.' Many readers of this book could, I am sure, tell other stories which exemplify just as dramatically the thrust of those two final petitions from the 'Our Father'.

For that matter, our newspapers bring us daily reports of various horrendous evils from which we pray to be delivered. Let me take an example from Africa, the Lord's Resistance Army who for years have abducted and killed at a rate that makes other terrorist groups seem tame. On 10 October 1996, these rebels in Uganda seized 139 girls from St Mary's College, one of the country's best Catholic boarding schools. An Italian nun, Sr Rachele Fassera, went into the night in search of the girls. The rebels agreed to release all but thirty of the girls. The nun pleaded with them and offered herself in place of the remaining girls. But the rebels refused and went off with their thirty captives. Over the years some of the thirty girls were killed and some have escaped. According to the last report, six of the St Mary's girls are believed to be still in captivity.

Reports on terrorist activities make it clear that the final petition of the 'Our Father' has lost nothing of its daily relevance. Reports on the environmental crisis also illustrate how timely that petition is. We seem to be approaching the point where the biological systems that support life on earth will collapse. The carbon dioxide emitted by cars has already polluted our atmosphere alarmingly. Over the last fifty years human beings have cut down over a third of our remaining forests, lost at least a quarter of the topsoil, and reduced the layer of ozone that protects us from excessive ultraviolet radiation. Greed and power, exercised for the chosen few, threaten to destroy us all. The environmental crisis has given a new edge to the prayer 'deliver us from evil', and to the drastic corrective actions that Christians and other human beings must take if we are to survive.

Part 4

◆

FURTHER CONSIDERATIONS

Chapter 12

♦

THE LORD'S PRAYER IN MARK AND JOHN

G IVEN THE IMPORTANCE OF the Lord's Prayer, it might seem odd that Mark and John do not include it. Yet those two gospels embody the spirit of the 'Our Father' and sometimes the letter. Let me begin with the Gospel of Mark which offers parallels to the language and seven petitions of the Lord's Prayer.

THE LORD'S PRAYER IN MARK

Mark's very first chapter highlights a striking manifestation of the Father. At the baptism of Jesus, the heavens are 'torn apart' and a voice from on high declares: 'You are my beloved Son; in you I am well pleased' (1:11). 'Our Father in the heavens' has spoken and will do so again at the transfiguration (9:7). In the Garden of Gethsemane Jesus prays to 'Abba, Father' (14:36). The Gospel of Mark should be read as the revelation of the divine identity of Jesus, which reaches its climax when the centurion confesses after the death of Jesus: 'Truly this man was the Son of God' (15:39). Revealing the divine sonship of Jesus obviously involves also revealing God 'in the heavens' to be Father or 'Abba'.

'May your name be made holy' may not enjoy a clear and direct parallel in Mark. Yet two items hint at this theme. Early in the gospel an evil spirit calls Jesus himself 'the Holy One of God' (1:24). Towards the end Jesus cleanses the Temple, the place of God's holy presence that has been defiled by trading (11:15–19).

There is much in Mark that matches the next petition in the Lord's Prayer: 'May your kingdom come'. The preaching of Jesus can be summed up as 'the kingdom of God is at hand' (1:15); it is a kingdom that is 'coming with power' (9:1). At the Last Supper Jesus promises 'to drink of the fruit of the vine' on 'that day' when he will drink it 'new in the kingdom of God' (14:25). The present and *coming* reign of God runs through the gospel, and not least in the discourse on 'the end of the age' (13:3–37).

The account of Jesus in Gethsemane echoes the Lord's Prayer with Jesus praying to 'Abba': 'not my will but your will be done' (14:36). We pick up here the petition 'may your will be done', just as we recognise 'do not bring us into temptation' in the words of Jesus to Peter and his companions, James and John: 'Keep awake and pray that you may not come into the time of trial' (14:38). The concern that the divine 'will be done' recurs repeatedly in Mark's gospel. It shows through the teaching of Jesus: for instance, his criticism of the traditions of the elders who risk setting details of ritual above the will of God (7:1–23), his insistence on the commandments of God (10:19), and his statement of the great commandment of love (12:28–34).

'Give us today our daily bread' does not occur as a prayer in Mark. Yet we can well see that petition dramatically fulfilled when, out of deep compassion for them, Jesus teaches and then miraculously feeds five thousand people who followed him to a 'deserted place'. The language used by the evangelist (and, most likely, the tradition on which he draws) applies to satisfying a need for basic food (bread and fish) through a miracle, but does so in ritual language that also suggests a eucharistic feeding. Jesus 'takes' the loaves and fish, 'looks up to heaven', 'blesses and breaks the loaves' and

116

'gives' them to be distributed (6:30–44). The material *and* spiritual sense of 'Give us today our daily bread' is exemplified brilliantly by Mark's story of five thousand people being taught and fed by Jesus.

The next petition in the Lord's Prayer, 'forgive us our debts as we also have forgiven our debtors', finds a partial counterpart in a major aspect of Jesus' ministry: the forgiveness of sins. Before healing a paralytic, Jesus absolves him of his sins (2:1–12). By dining with Levi and many other 'tax collectors and sinners', Jesus expresses his mission to forgive sinful human beings and arouses criticism from the self-righteous. He reacts by picturing himself as a doctor to the sick and insists: 'I have come to call not the righteous but sinners' (2:13–17). Mark's gospel also indicates that receiving divine forgiveness is conditioned by our willingness to forgive others. In the words of Jesus, 'Whenever you stand praying, forgive, if you have anything against any one; so that your Father also who is in heaven may forgive you your trespasses' (Mark 11:25).

Then the plea, 'Do not bring us into temptation', has its clear Marcan counterpart not only, as we saw above, in something Jesus says to the disciples in Gethsemane (14:38), but also in the example of Jesus himself. After his baptism 'he was in the wilderness forty days, tempted by Satan' (1:13); evidently one is meant to understand that Jesus did not succumb to the tempter. A few chapters later, the explanation of the parable of the sower warns against the danger of 'falling away' when 'trouble or persecution arises on account of the word' (4:17) – a warning that is developed in terms of the tribulations that will come at the end of the age (13:3–37). Mark's gospel seems to be addressed to Christians who have been suffering persecution, and need to be encouraged to follow in the footsteps of a crucified Master. In a powerful fashion that theme develops over several chapters (8:14—10:52), ending with the striking case of Bartimaeus. After receiving his sight, he does something that no other person in this gospel does when cured by Jesus. Bartimaeus 'follows' Jesus and does so 'on the way' leading up to Jerusalem – the way of the cross that begins in 'the villages of Caesarea Philippi' (8:27), leads south 'through Galilee' (9:30), into 'the region of Judaea' (10:1), and then takes Jesus 'on the road going up to Jerusalem' (10:32), the place of his passion and death. If they are not to succumb to temptation, Christians need to have their eyes opened by Jesus. Then like Bartimaeus they will be enabled to prove to be his faithful followers and not fail in time of tribulation.

Finally, we have seen in the last chapter how Mark's gospel, especially through the expulsion of evil spirits, illustrates the concluding petition of the Lord's Prayer, 'deliver us from the evil one'. In particular, no other episode in any of the four gospels comments more eloquently on this plea than Mark's lengthy story of Jesus delivering the Gerasene demoniac.

THE LORD'S PRAYER IN JOHN

John's gospel may be read as one long prayer; it comes out of decades of prayer and easily leads back into prayer. One might interpret it as a great act of contemplation that sweeps from the community's response at the beginning to an individual's act of adoration at the end: from 'the Word became flesh ... and we have contemplated his glory' (1:14), to the confession of Thomas, 'My Lord and my God' (20:28). One might also understand this gospel to unpack the Lord's Prayer. Its themes are there, even if the text as such is not.

John's gospel names God as 'Father' 118 times (with two uncertain further references). The first time it does so reproduces something of the intimacy with which the Lord's Prayer opens: 'God the only Son, who is close to the Father's heart, has made him known' (1:18). That opening reference to the Father sets the tone for the prayerful presence of the Father right through the Fourth Gospel. That presence reaches its climax in the high priestly prayer of Jesus (17:1–26), which addresses the Father six times and begins with Jesus 'looking up to heaven and saying, "Father, the hour has come, glorify your Son so that the Son may glorify you".'

The equivalent of 'May your name be made holy' occurs at the end of the public ministry when Jesus is troubled by the approach of his passion and prays: 'Father, glorify your name' (12:28).

Here, as elsewhere in John's gospel, it is Jesus himself who shows what it is to pray the 'Our Father'. Jesus enacts over and over again the text that, according to Matthew and Luke, he left as a prayer for his followers.

Apart from speaking to Nicodemus about seeing and entering the kingdom of God (3:3–5), Jesus hardly mentions the kingdom in the Fourth Gospel and never asks his followers to pray, 'may your kingdom come'. It is Jesus himself who replaces the kingdom; he is the kingdom in person. Instead of preaching the kingdom of God, he identifies himself – most spectacularly in the 'I am' sayings: 'I am the bread of life'; 'I am the light of the world'; 'I am the way, the truth, and the life'; and 'before Abraham was made, I am'. Instead of talking of the coming kingdom, Jesus promises, in a most consoling fashion, that he will come again and take us to himself, so that where he is, we also may be (14:3). In brief, it is Jesus who is the kingdom, already present and still to come.

In place of the petition 'may your will be done', Jesus himself enacts the divine will. He is the 'doer' par excellence of the will of God. Repeatedly he witnesses to his personal obedience to the Father: 'the one who sent me is with me; he has not left me alone, for I always do what is pleasing to him' (8:29). The life of Jesus in John's gospel, even more clearly than in the other gospels, is a story of loving obedience to the Father and his will.

We have already seen above (Chapter 8) how John's long discourse on Jesus as 'the bread of life' forms the best commentary on the petition 'Give us today our daily bread'. Both here and hereafter Jesus is life-giving sustenance to all who accept him: 'Those who eat my flesh and drink my blood have eternal life, and I will raise them up on the last day' (6:54). On the night before Jesus dies, the Fourth Gospel introduces the image of the vine and its branches, another way of symbolising the fruitful function of Jesus for those who seek life through and in him.

Jesus, who has been named as 'the Lamb of God who takes away the sin of the world' (1:29), calls for an honest recognition of one's sins. He admonishes those who refuse to admit their spiritual blindness: 'If you were blind, you would not have sin. But now that you say, "We see", your sin remains' (9:41). Unbelief blinds people to their sins (8:24, 34). Both in his earthly ministry (5:14) and when risen from the dead (20:23), Jesus is concerned for repentance and the forgiveness of sins. Does he see such forgiveness as conditioned by our forgiving attitude towards others – in the spirit of 'forgive us our debts as we also have forgiven our debtors'? Certainly he calls his disciples to love one another as he has loved them (15:12). Since forgiveness embodies love, at times heroic love, we find in the Fourth Gospel an equivalent to the petition in the Lord's Prayer for a forgiveness from God that finds its counterpart in our forgiving the sins others may have committed against us.

Jesus' farewell discourse (14:1—17:26) contains warnings of the severe testing and even failures of his close followers. Thus he warns Peter of an imminent failure: 'before the cock crows, you will have denied me three times' (13:38). He predicts that his servants will be tested by persecutions, violence and even death (15:18–21; 16:1–4). But they can 'take courage', since Jesus has 'conquered the world' (16:33). They will find themselves in situations of drastic trials, but can always be sure of the powerful presence of the risen Christ and the Holy Spirit. In that way the farewell discourse in John incorporates and goes beyond the plea, 'Do not bring us into temptation.'

Unlike the other gospels, John includes no stories of demons being expelled by Jesus, stories which respond in

120

action to the closing petition of the Lord's Prayer, 'deliver us from the evil one'. Yet Satan is far from absent in the Fourth Gospel. Jesus uses strong language about him when confronting critics: 'You are from your father, the devil ... He was a murderer from the beginning and does not stand in the truth, because there is no truth in him ... He is a liar and the father of lies' (John 8:44). Thus John fills out what we wish to be delivered from when we pray, 'deliver us from the evil one'. No less than in the other gospels, the Jesus of the Fourth Gospel is in the business of delivering people from lies and death by giving them the truth and the fullness of life.

In the Introduction I referred to all those Christians who down through the centuries have translated and interpreted the Lord's Prayer. The text itself is found in Matthew and Luke. The process of translating and interpreting this most precious prayer begins already with Mark and John.

Chapter 13

◆

'FOR YOURS IS THE KINGDOM, THE POWER AND THE GLORY'

IN THE INTRODUCTION WE saw how a very early Christian document treasured the Lord's Prayer and recommended its use three times a day. The *Didache*, which was composed around the time when the last books of the NT were being written, helped to launch this prayer into its flourishing life in preaching, catechesis, different kinds of usage in the liturgy, and private devotional practice. The *Didache* also helped to initiate the process of rounding off the Lord's Prayer with the words, 'for yours is the kingdom, the power and the glory'.

These words of praise or 'doxology' represent both loss and gain. For those who agree with the translation 'deliver us from the evil one', the Lord's Prayer moves from the loving, truthful Father to the evil one, the false murderous father. This view of the prayer as a kind of 'tale of two fathers' finds an echo in the words that Jesus addresses in John's gospel to those who plan to kill him: 'You are from your father the devil, and you choose to do your father's desires. He was a murderer from the beginning and does not stand in the truth, because there is no truth in him ... he is a liar and the father of lies' (John 8:44). Seen this way, the Lord's Prayer is bracketed in a startling fashion by two 'fathers'. It opens by invoking the utterly compassionate and real Father in the heavens and ends with a plea to be delivered from Satan, the evil father of lies and primordial murderer.

In the light of what we glean from his teaching, Jesus could easily have presented such a stark contrast in the prayer that he gave to his disciples. For instance, he personified wealth and bluntly told his audience: 'No one can serve two masters; for a servant will either hate the one and love the other, or be devoted to the one and despise the other. You cannot serve God and Mammon' (Matt. 6:24; parallel in Luke 16:13). The Lord's Prayer suggests a similar plain choice: you cannot love and serve both your heavenly Father and the diabolic father of lies. There can be no compromise here. You must be utterly devoted to 'Abba' and pray to be delivered from the counterfeit, murderous father, the devil.

It might have been because they found it hard to move from naming their heavenly Father to ending with Satan that early Christians eventually added the doxology to the Lord's Prayer, 'for yours is the kingdom, the power and the glory for ever and ever. Amen.' Or perhaps they were driven more by the desire to add a decorous and solemn conclusion by invoking three powerful biblical themes: the kingdom, power and glory which all belong eternally to God.

By making 'glory' the climax of the triad (kingdom, power and glory), those responsible for this addition echoed a sentiment that we find in the psalms and that has received some exquisite musical settings from William Byrd (1543–1623) and other great composers: 'non nobis, Domine, non nobis, sed nomini tuo da gloriam (not to us, Lord, not to us, but to your name give glory)'. All glory goes to God rather than to any of our merits or merely human achievements.

The gain that the doxology represents has been amply vindicated in the story of Christian liturgy. From the early centuries, the liturgies of Eastern Christians incorporated it and in the West it came massively into its own at the time of the Reformation. John Calvin regarded the doxology as an integral part of the Lord's Prayer. Even if Martin Luther was reluctant to introduce the doxology into his liturgical texts, it soon appeared anyway in Lutheran worship. In the aftermath of the Second Vatican Council it has been incorporated in the Latin Mass as 'for the kingdom, the power, and the glory are yours, now and forever'.

Among its 'you' petitions the Lord's Prayer includes the words 'May your kingdom come'. By picking up again the theme of 'the kingdom', the final doxology drives home a theme of central importance. The 'Our Father' concerns the kingdom, and can properly be described as *the* prayer of the kingdom. There is, of course, another way of summarising its thrust. In the oldest commentary we have on the Lord's Prayer, Tertullian described it as 'an epitome of the whole Gospel (*breviarium totius evangelii*)' (*De oratione* 1). Yet this amounts to the same conviction. After all, in a programmatic statement that opens the public ministry in Mark's gospel, Jesus declares: 'the *kingdom* of God is at hand; repent and believe in the *Gospel* (good news)' (Mark 1:15). The kingdom of God is the Gospel, and the good news par excellence is the kingdom.

The Lord's Prayer summarises the message of the kingdom and of the Gospel. We can do nothing less than treasure it with deep thanks and say it or sing it with quiet devotion.

♦

NOTES

INTRODUCTION

1. E. Muir, *An Autobiography* (London: Methuen, 1964), p. 246.
2. Origen, *Treatise on Prayer* 18.3, trans. E. G. Jay (London: SPCK, 1954), pp. 136–8.
3. See J. P. Meier, *A Marginal Jew: Rethinking the Historical Jesus*, vol. 2 (New York: Doubleday, 1994), p. 355.
4. Jesus did not (and could not) pray 'forgive us our sins', but we find him addressing God as 'Abba' and praying 'your will be done' (Mark 14:36) and (equivalently) 'may your name be made holy' (John 12:28).
5. The setting of prayer that Luke provides here corresponds to what he does elsewhere. Prayer precedes or accompanies other highly significant moments in the story of Jesus: such as the baptism (Luke 3:21), the call of the Twelve (Luke 6:12) and the transfiguration (Luke 9:29). It is implied that what Jesus shares about his own prayer life (Luke 11:1–4) stands on a similar level of importance with those earlier episodes.

1: STARTING WITH 'ABBA'

1. See G. O'Collins and D. Kendall, *The Bible for Theology* (Mahwah, NJ: Paulist Press, 1997), pp. 93–6.
2. M. Z. Brettler, *God Is King: Understanding an Israelite Metaphor* (Sheffield: JSOT Press, 1989), p. 60.
3. Despite his extraordinary knowledge of the scriptures, Origen was to miss this and some other passages (which we will see) when he commented that in the OT nobody 'addresses God as Father': *Treatise on Prayer* 22.1, trans. E. G. Jay (London: SPCK, 1954), p. 144. The address is highly unusual, but not unknown.

4. G. Vermes, *The Dead Sea Scrolls in English* (Harmondsworth: Penguin Books, 3rd edn, 1987), p. 192 (IQH 9.34–35).
5. See G. D. Fee, *God's Empowering Presence: The Holy Spirit in the Letters of Paul* (Peabody, MA: Hendrickson, 1994), pp. 410–12; J. P. Meier, *A Marginal Jew*, vol. 2 (New York: Doubleday, 1994), pp. 358–89. Famously (or notoriously?) Joachim Jeremias years ago claimed that 'abba', like 'imma', derived from children's speech ('Dada' and 'Mama'): *The Prayers of Jesus* (London: SCM Press, 1967), p. 58. James Barr challenged this position, but admitted that *'abba* in Jesus' time belonged to a familiar or colloquial register of language, as distinct from more formal or ceremonious usage': 'Abba isn't "Daddy"', *Journal of Theological Studies* 39 (1988), 28–47, at 46.
6. When reporting the prayer of Jesus in Gethsemane, Matthew and Luke do not reproduce the Marcan 'Abba', just as they drop other Aramaic expressions that Mark records (Mark 3:17; 5:41; 7:11; 11:34; 15:34). The only Marcan Aramaisms that survive in either Matthew or Luke are 'Hosanna' (Mark 11:9–10; parallel in Matt. 21:9) and 'Golgotha' (Mark 15:22; parallel in Matt. 27:33).
7. J. D. G. Dunn, *Christology in the Making* (London: SCM Press, 2nd edn, 1989), p. 27; see also *Jesus Remembered* (Grand Rapids, MI: Eerdmans, 2003), pp. 248–53, 717.
8. See the discussion of Matthew 11:25–30 in D. A. Hagner, *Matthew 1—13*, Word Biblical Commentary, vol. 33a (Dallas: Word Books, 1993), pp. 315–21; on the parallel in Luke 10:21–22, see J. A. Fitzmyer, *The Gospel according to Luke X—XXIV*, Anchor Bible, vol. 28a (Garden City, NY: Doubleday, 1985), pp. 864–76.
9. On the Lord's Prayer in Matthew and Luke, see Fitzmyer, *Luke X—XXIV*, pp. 896–908; J. Nolland, *Luke 9:21—18: 34*, Word Biblical Commentary, vol. 35b (Dallas: Word Books, 1993), pp. 607–21; Meier, *A Marginal Jew*, vol. 2, pp. 291–302, 353–60, 363–4.
10. Ancient Judaism displayed no uniform system of messianic expectation. Along with the dominant notion of a Davidic Messiah or ruler who would restore the kingdom of Israel, there were minor messianic strands that included a priestly messiah, an anointed prophet, and a heavenly Son of Man. The figures promised in ancient Judaism were not necessarily anointed and so 'messianic'; conversely, someone who was anointed and so 'messianic' was not necessarily an eschatological or end-time figure (e.g. Ps. 45:7). In particular, pre-Christian Judaism left no evidence that 'a/the Son of God' or 'son of God' was ever regarded as *messianic*, in the sense of being expected as the future, anointed agent of God. On the evidence for 'Son of God' emerging as a messianic title right at the time of Jesus, see my *Christology: A Biblical, Historical, and Systematic Study*

of Jesus (Oxford: Oxford University Press, rev. edn, 2004), pp. 115–18.

11. See Tertullian, *De Oratione* 2–3, ed. and trans. E. Evans (London: SPCK, 1953), pp. 5–6.

12. See P. Widdicombe, *The Fatherhood of God from Origen to Athanasius* (Oxford: Clarendon Press, 1994).

2: SAVING 'ABBA'

1. See D. A. Hagner, *Matthew 1—13*, vol. 33a (Dallas: Word Books, 1993), pp. 126–9; C. S. Keener, *A Commentary on the Gospel of Matthew* (Grand Rapids, MI: Eerdmans, 1999), pp. 92–5.

2. On going beyond the (literal) meaning of authors, see G. O'Collins, *Easter Faith* (London: Darton, Longman & Todd, 2003), pp. 81–4.

3. In his *Tractates on the Gospel of John*, Augustine exclaimed, 'Show me a lover and he will understand' (26.4).

4. R. E. Brown, *The Death of the Messiah*, vol. 1 (New York: Doubleday, 1994), p. 174.

5. See G. O'Collins, 'Images of Jesus: Reappropriating Titular Christology', *Theology Digest* 44 (1997), 303–18.

6. Paul's standard greeting in his letters was: 'grace and peace from God our Father and the Lord Jesus Christ' (e.g. Rom. 1:7). As well as using this greeting in opening his Second Letter to the Corinthians, the Apostle added: 'Praise be to the God and Father of our Lord Jesus Christ, the Father of mercies and the God of all comfort, who comfort us in all our troubles' (2 Cor. 1:3–4). Paul characterises the Father as the source of grace, peace, mercy and comfort.

7. On household codes, see H. Moxnes (ed.), *Constructing Early Christian Families* (London: Routledge, 1997); C. Osiek and D. L. Balch, *Families in the New Testament World: Households and Household Churches* (Louisville, KY: Westminster/John Knox, 1997).

3: 'OUR FATHER'

1. C. Houselander, *This War is the Passion* (London: Sheed and Ward, 1943), pp. 61–2; text slightly edited. Psalm 31:5 says: 'Into your hand I commit my spirit; you have redeemed me, O Lord, faithful God.' Either Jesus or Luke (or Luke's source at this point) added 'Father'.

4: 'IN THE HEAVENS'

1. See G. O'Collins, *The Second Journey* (Leominster: Gracewing, 3rd edn, 1995).

2. See Diana Webb, *Pilgrims and Pilgrimages in the Medieval West* (London: Tauris, 1999).

5: 'MAY YOUR NAME BE MADE HOLY'

1. John's gospel expresses this point equivalently in the prayer of Jesus, 'Father, glorify your name' (12:28).

6: 'MAY YOUR KINGDOM COME'

1. Two lawyers informed me that in certain countries today someone who concealed his find and bought the property from a freeholder could be sued later for not having declared his discovery. The law in the Middle East of Jesus' time did not seem to impose such obligations on fortunate finders. Nevertheless, while not legally obliged to report his discovery, the treasure-finder knew that he had to buy the field, if he were to keep the treasure without being challenged.

8: 'GIVE US TODAY OUR DAILY BREAD'

1. Thomas G. Casey, *Humble and Awake: Coping with our Comatose Culture* (Springfield, IL: Templegate, 2004), p. 48.
2. St Jerome in his commentary on Matthew, written in 383, followed Origen's interpretation and translated *epiousios* as *supersubstantialis* ('necessary to support life'). This clumsy word was inserted in the influential Latin Vulgate Bible. Fortunately the Roman liturgy continued to use (from the Old Latin version) the flexible *quotidianum*, which could mean 'daily', 'for today', 'for existence', 'for our needs', 'for the coming day' or 'for the future'.
3. A. J. Bradley (ed.), *Anglo-Saxon Poetry* (London: Dent, 1982), p. 534; translation adjusted.
4. St Cyprian, *The Lord's Prayer*, in *Saint Cyprian Treatises*, trans. R. J. Deferrari (Washington, DC: Catholic University of America Press, 1958), pp. 125–59, at pp. 142–6.
5. St Gregory of Nyssa, *The Lord's Prayer, the Beatitudes*, trans. H. C. Graef (New York: Newman Press, 1954), pp. 21–84, at pp. 63–70.
6. St Augustine of Hippo, *Commentary on the Lord's Sermon on the Mount*, trans. D. J. Kavanagh (Washington: Catholic University of America Press, 1951), p. 135.
7. The gospels provide no story of any conversion of Mary Magdalene. Luke lists her first among the women whom Jesus had cured of 'evil spirits and infirmities' and adds that 'seven demons had gone out of her' (Luke 8:2–3).

9: 'FORGIVE US OUR DEBTS, AS WE ALSO HAVE FORGIVEN OUR DEBTORS'

1. A. Camus, *The Fall*, trans. Justin O'Brien (London: Penguin, 2000), p. 60.
2. In his 1536 translation of Matthew's version of the Lord's Prayer,

Miles Coverdale used 'debts' and 'debtors' for the forgiveness petition. It was the 1534 translation by William Tyndale, however, that made 'trespass' standard throughout the world of English-speaking Christians: 'and forgive us our trespasses, even as we forgive our trespassers'. (I put Tyndale's words into modern spelling.)

10: 'DO NOT BRING US INTO TEMPTATION'

1. Hebrews 4:15 recalls that Jesus was 'in every respect tested/tempted as we are, yet without sin'. Through telling the story of the temptations in the desert, the gospels spell out the form this testing took at the start of Jesus' ministry. They do the same through their account of his agonising struggle in the Garden of Gethsemane, to which Hebrews briefly alludes (5:7–8).
2. *Treatise on Prayer*, trans. E. G. Jay (London: SPCK, 1954), p. 196.

BIBLIOGRAPHY

With special interest in its liturgical usage, Bishop Kenneth Stevenson has included a great deal of exciting bibliographical material on the 'Our Father' in *The Lord's Prayer: Text and Tradition* (Minneapolis: Augsburg Fortress Publishers, 2004).

From a biblical point of view, John P. Meier not only comments on the Lord's Prayer but also offers a valuable bibliography in *A Marginal Jew: Rethinking the Historical Jesus*, vol. 2 (New York: Doubleday, 1994), pp. 291–302, 353–60, 363–4.

Long commentaries on Matthew's gospel discuss in detail the text of the Lord's Prayer. See, for instance, D. A. Hagner, *Matthew 1—13*, Word Biblical Commentary, vol. 33a (Dallas: Word Books, 1993); C. S. Keener, *A Commentary on the Gospel of Matthew* (Grand Rapids, MI: Eerdmans, 1999).

Even though they deal only with the briefer Lucan version (Luke 11:2–4), standard commentaries on Luke's gospel yield valuable material on the Lord's Prayer. See, for instance, D. L. Bock, *Luke, Volume 2: 9:51—24:53* (Grand Rapids, MI: Baker Books, 1996); J. A. Fitzmyer, *The Gospel According to Luke X—XXIV*, Anchor Bible 28a (Garden City, NY: Doubleday, 1985); J. Nolland, *Luke 18:35—24:53*, Word Biblical Commentary, vol. 35c (Dallas: Word Books, 1993).

The Catechism of the Catholic Church (different editions since it was first published in 1992) ends with a long section on the Lord's Prayer (nos. 2759–2865), which contains illuminating material from the scriptures and the fathers of the Church.

◆

INDEX OF NAMES